THE
DOOMSDAY
MYTH

THE DOOMSDAY MYTH

10,000 Years of Economic Crises

CHARLES MAURICE

CHARLES W. SMITHSON

FOREWORD BY PHIL GRAMM

HOOVER INSTITUTION PRESS
Stanford University
Stanford, California

The following publishers have generously given permission to use extended selections from the following works: John U. Nef, "An Early Energy Crisis and Its Consequences," *Scientific American*, November 1977, pp. 140–51, reprinted by permission of W. H. Freeman and Company; John U. Nef, *The Rise of the British Coal Industry* (London, 1966), reprinted by permission of Frank Cass & Co. Ltd.

The cartoons in Chapter 1 are reprinted by permission of Mike Peters, *Dayton Daily News*, and Hugh Haynie and *The Courier-Journal*, Louisville, Ky.

Portions of the present work appeared in Charles Maurice and Charles Smithson, *Are We Running Out of Everything*, Series on Public Issues, no. 1 (College Station: Center for Education and Research in Free Enterprise, Texas A&M University, 1983).

Hoover Press Publication 296
Copyright 1984 by the Board of Trustees of the
    Leland Stanford Junior University
First printing, 1984. First paperback printing, 1987.
Manufactured in the United States of America
88 87   9 8 7 6 5

Library of Congress Cataloging in Publication Data
Maurice, S. Charles.
    The doomsday myth.

    Bibliography: p.
    1. Scarcity. 2. Substitution (Economics) 3. Natural resources.
4. Power resources. 5. Laissez-faire. I. Smithson, C. W.
(Charles W.) II. Title
HB199.M35   1984   330.9   84-3757
ISBN 0-8179-7961-1
ISBN 0-8179-7962-X (pbk.)

Design by P. Kelley Baker

To the faculty of Texas A&M University,
without whom this book would not
have been begun and certainly
would never have been completed

CONTENTS

LIST OF TABLES

LIST OF FIGURES

FOREWORD

IN the course of the debate that has raged concerning the energy policy of the United States and our general policies regarding natural resources, one point seems to have been accepted by the vast majority of the participants: government must do something. The only point left open to debate seems to have been how much government should do. And all too frequently the answer I have heard is "The more the better."

Why is it that Americans have come to expect that the government should be required to intervene in such a situation? Is this the result of history's teaching us that only government can eliminate resource shortages? In this book, Charles Maurice and Charles Smithson look at some historical experiences that indicate that government has not in the past been very successful in eliminating resource shortages. Indeed, their conclusion is that the working of an unfettered marketplace rather than some government planner has eliminated the resource shortages that have been experienced in the past.

During the 1970s, when the price of oil was rising so rapidly and we experienced those seemingly endless gasoline lines or shortages of heating oil, we frequently heard such statements as:

"A new age of scarcity is here."

"We've got to learn to live with less—a lot less."

"This is the end of society as we know it."

"Someone has to protect us from our wasteful ways."

This book shows that it "just ain't so." This isn't a new age of scarcity. We don't need to be protected from our wasteful, wasteful ways. We don't have to learn to live with less. The authors point out that what happened in the 1970s has happened before. Indeed, the experiences of the 1970s have been happening for centuries.

Societies have experienced resource shortages throughout history, many as bad as and some worse than the petroleum shortages in the 1970s. The amazing thing demonstrated by Maurice and Smithson is that government programs didn't solve these resource crises. The crises ended because markets work—people reacted to the higher prices of the scarce resource by finding substitutes for the scarce resource, by adopting new technologies, and by price-induced conservation. This is the way the market worked in the 1970s, and the way it has worked for the past 10,000 years.

To tell their story, the authors begin by showing how deregulation brought about the solution to our recent energy crisis. As we all are happily aware, after deregulation, we went from oil shortages to an oil glut. Once the price system was again permitted to function, consumers and producers reacted to the high price of petroleum and eliminated the shortage. It was the elimination of governmentally imposed controls—not the institution of a new government program—that eliminated the so-called energy crisis.

But this is only the beginning of their story—or, more correctly, only our most recent experience with resource shortages. Maurice and Smithson take us back through history to show how often the same scenario has been played. Freely functioning markets, with consumers and producers adapting to higher prices, have solved several "resource crises" in America—the natural rubber crisis of 1942, the great timber crisis at the turn of the century, and the whale oil crisis of the 1850s.

Crossing the Atlantic, the authors show that it was again the marketplace that solved England's timber crisis—and that was a serious crisis—in the years prior to its industrial revolution. Even earlier, the working of the marketplace was responsible for eliminating the problems of the labor shortages that resulted from the sweep of the plagues through Europe in the fourteenth century.

Even the ancient civilizations were not exempt from resource crises. The ancient Greeks experienced a severe shortage in bronze—a material that was as "essential" to their civilization as petroleum is to ours. Again, it was the market that eliminated this shortage and set the stage for the beginning of the Iron Age. Even primitive man experienced resource shortages, and, as Maurice and Smithson demonstrate, the way they solved their shortages was precisely the way we solved our petroleum shortage.

So, the lesson that Maurice and Smithson present is that nothing much has changed in the past 10,000 years. If consumers and producers are left to work out agreements in a freely functioning market, resource shortages—"crises"—will always be eliminated. It happened in the 1970s, and it has happened for more than a hundred centuries. The solution to the energy crisis and the way that the market place has been able to solve resource crises as far back as the Stone Age are nothing short of miraculous! What a paradox it is then that we are so quick to look to government for solutions to our economic problems, when governments have provided so few solutions, and that we have been so slow to turn to the market, which has proved to be a faithful servant.

Think about the energy crisis for a moment. As recently as 1980, many self-styled experts were saying that we were going to be totally at the mercy of OPEC for generations to come. Look what happened in such a very short period of time. And it is essential to remember that the problem was solved in spite of—rather than because of—the activities of our government. This was a miracle, even though no one speaks of it as such. The problem is that many people view our recovery as some sort of a lucky accident. So we continue to hear people calling for government to "do something."

Maurice and Smithson show that this miraculous recovery was not an isolated accident. The miracle has occurred many times in the past. In fact it has occurred every time there has been a resource crisis in the past, so long as there was little governmental interference with a freely functioning market.

Just as great a miracle happened at the beginning of World War II, when the Japanese captured practically all of the world's supply of natural rubber. Within a very short time, the United States was manufacturing all of the synthetic rubber it needed to fight a war. And this massive technological change was not the result of a government research program (despite the myth that our government was somehow responsible for the invention of synthetic rubber). Quite the contrary. As Maurice and Smithson demonstrate, this crisis was solved by the market reaction to a cartel years before—a situation not unlike our recent experience with OPEC. The development of synthetic rubber was a miracle brought about by the marketplace.

And I could go on to list the other miracles that Maurice and Smithson have described—although they did not describe them as such. Let me limit myself to only one more. The introduction of petroleum as an energy source in America was itself a miracle. Without it, much of what we have accomplished in the past hundred years would have been impossible. And this miracle was again the outcome of a freely functioning market. The search for oil was not the result of the actions of a group of altruists. Instead, the search for petroleum was the result of an energy crisis: we were running out of the traditional energy source in America—whale oil.

Maurice and Smithson recount for us in this book many examples that make but a single point: economic freedom has been the key to our progress in the past, and it is the key to our progress in the future. If we can preserve economic freedom, there is no limit to the future of mankind. Great nations and great civilizations do not die by consuming their resource base. They die by consuming their institutions and their freedoms, and, in the process, they render themselves incapable of finding solutions to the problems that face them.

PHIL GRAMM

U.S. House of Representatives
Washington, D.C.

PREFACE

> If the present rate of [*petroleum*] con-
> sumption is allowed to continue . . . a
> [*petroleum*] famine in the future is
> inevitable.

DOESN'T that sound familiar? During the past decade, we have constantly been told by self-styled experts that we are running out of oil. However, the preceding quote was not from the 1970s and the speaker was not talking about petroleum. This quote was discovered by Sherry H. Olson in a speech made in 1905 by President Theodore Roosevelt. In this speech, President Roosevelt was talking about *timber* rather than *petroleum*. In the early 1900s, Roosevelt and many other public officials and experts were concerned about a timber crisis. And, from this quotation and others, it appears that they were as concerned about this timber crisis as we were about our energy crisis of the 1970s.

President Roosevelt's dismal prediction is not unique. Similar predictions have been made throughout recorded history. The only difference has been which resource we were running out of. Most recently, it was petroleum. In 1905, it was timber. In other eras, there have been other critical resources—food, rubber, whale oil, charcoal, labor, and tin, to name just a few. And in each instance, there have been experts who predicted that we were soon to run out of the resource and that society was doomed.

Forecasts of doom and gloom have existed for as long as civilization has existed. The important fact is, however, that all of these forecasts of doom have been wrong. No civilization has collapsed due to the depletion of a resource. Instead, freely functioning markets with people acting in their own self interest have eliminated the shortages.

This then is the theme of our book: if markets are given the freedom to respond, people will react to shortages and the resulting increases in prices with substitution and/or technological change, thereby eliminating the crisis. Our theme is the same one used by Adam Smith in 1776 in *The Wealth of Nations*. The idea is an old one, but the need to restate it is as new as the editorial pages of today's newspapers.

In the popular press, we have been told that "this is a whole new ballgame" or "this problem is different" or "this problem demands different solutions." But the problems we face today are not different from those we have experienced in the past. We are not in a whole new ballgame. The shortage—or crisis—game has been played many times before, with the same result. In this book, we present historical evidence—some from this century, some from antiquity, and some in between—to show that the pattern of resource scarcity and adaptation has consistently recurred. We then use that historical evidence to argue that as long as markets are permitted to function freely we can expect the same type of response to future resource crises.

In that light, this book should be regarded as an essay reflecting our understanding of the workings of markets. We sincerely believe that the power of the marketplace can and will continue to eliminate shortages and protect us from cut-offs by foreign suppliers. However, over the past years, we have had a difficult time communicating our optimism to others, try as we would. This difficulty was especially evident in 1979. Faced with long gasoline lines and rapidly rising prices, most people were simply unwilling to accept our argument that a return to an unregulated petroleum market would end the shortage and result in lower gasoline prices. It was then that we began to rely on the stories we are about to relate to you.

Our faith in the ability of the market to eliminate crises is not based on metaphysics or even on the power of modern economic theory. Instead, it is based on the simple fact that the market has worked to eliminate resource shortages in the past. More specifically, since the marketplace has worked for the past ten thousand years why should we expect that it will not work in the future?

To illustrate how the market has worked in the past, we are going to tell you about ten major economic crises mankind has experienced. In the context of our essay, we have selected what we feel are some of the more important crises. In order to highlight the most important issues, we have simplified some of the discussion. (But our sources are available if you wish to read more about a specific crisis.) Furthermore, this is not an academic tome. We did not do any primary research in the sense of reading manorial records from the Middle Ages or examining archaeological artifacts. Instead, we relied upon secondary but, we feel, reliable sources. We have attempted to summarize what others have written to show how the market has worked to solve the crises.

Neither of us is a historian. In the vein of former senator Sam Ervin's famous statement, we are just simple, country economists. We owe a great debt to those who helped us with this project. Of course, none of these individuals who helped us can be held responsible for the final content of this book. Indeed, some of them do not—yet— share our optimistic view of a market economy. (But we are still working on them.) As is so often the case with a book having two authors, each of us blames the other for any errors.

ACKNOWLEDGMENTS

WE are deeply indebted to many people for their support and assistance. In particular we wish to acknowledge:

WILLIAM BREIT
Department of
Economics
Trinity University

JOHN R. HANSON, II
Department of
Economics
Texas A&M University

VAUGHN M. BRYANT
Department of Sociology
Texas A&M University

WILLA ANN JOHNSON
Heritage Foundation
Washington, D.C.

CHESTER S.L. DUNNING
Department of History
Texas A&M University

DALE T. KNOBEL
Department of History
Texas A&M University

ROBERT B. EKELUND, JR.
Department of
Economics
Auburn University

HUGH H. MACAULAY
Department of
Economics
Clemson University

PHIL GRAMM
U.S. House of
Representatives
Washington, D.C.

RICHARD B. McKENZIE
Department of
Economics
Clemson University

JOHN H. MOORE
Hoover Institution on War,
    Revolution and Peace
Stanford, California

SVETOZAR PEJOVICH
Center for Research and
    Education in Free
    Enterprise
Texas A&M University

ROBERT POOLE, JR.
Reason Foundation
Santa Barbara,
    California

ED RIFKIN
Bureau of Economics
Federal Trade Commission

BRUCE E. SEELEY
Department of History
Texas A&M University

HARRY J. SHAFER
Archaeology and
    Anthropology Program
Texas A&M University

DAVID THAYER
El Paso Products Co.
Odessa, Texas

ROBERT TOLLISON
Department of
    Economics
Clemson University

D. SYKES WILFORD
Chase Manhattan Bank
New York, New York

RICHARD ZECHER
Chase Manhattan Bank
New York, New York

Last, but by no means least, we wish to thank Tricia Ofczarzak and
Dale Bremmer for their assistance in the research for and preparation
of this manuscript. Without them, this project would have remained a
collection of ideas written on scraps of paper.

THE
DOOMSDAY
MYTH

THE ENERGY CRISIS IS OVER!

1

WHO in 1979 would have believed that by the early 1980s our concern with energy would have diminished to such an extent? How do you suppose a person waiting in one of those enormous gasoline lines would have reacted to the suggestion that by 1983 we would be talking about the collapse of OPEC and the "problems" of a rapidly falling petroleum price? Confronted with odd/even rationing and red flags signaling that service stations had no more gasoline to sell, how many people would have believed that in a span of only four years gasoline stations would once again be handing out glassware in order to attract customers?

Looking back over the period 1972–1983, we find the changes in public sentiment concerning energy to be nothing short of amazing. Permit us to review this cycle in public opinion as it was reflected in the headlines of some of the most widely read periodicals.

1972   "U.S. ENERGY STILL ABUNDANT. . . ," *New York Times*, January 9

1973   "WHO SHUT THE HEAT OFF?" *Time*, February 12

"SUMMER 1973: THE ECONOMICS OF SCARCITY," *Newsweek*, July 9

We take our title for this chapter and parts of the discussion from an excellent article by William Tucker that appeared in the November 1981 issue of *Harper's*.

1974	"ENERGY: HOW HIGH IS UP?" *Newsweek* (cover story), January 7
1975	"ENERGY CONSERVATION IS BECOMING A HABIT," *New York Times*, October 30
1976	"AUTOS: THINKING NOT SO SMALL," *Newsweek*, March 1
	"BACK ON A DANGEROUS BINGE," *Time*, August 30
1977	"YES, THERE *IS* AN ENERGY CRISIS," *Time*, October 10
1978	"ENERGY: WHERE DID THE CRISIS GO?" *New York Times*, April 16
1979	"A LONG DRY SUMMER," *Newsweek* (cover story), April 21
	"OVER A BARREL," *Newsweek* (cover story), July 9
1980	"GASOLINE GAUGES REST ON FULL," *Time*, July 28
1981	"THE GOOD NEWS ABOUT OIL," *Newsweek*, April 27
1982	"DOWN, DOWN, DOWN: OPEC FINDS THAT IT IS A CRUDE, CRUDE WORLD," *Time*, March 15
	"OPEC TRIES AGAIN TO SOP UP THE GLUT," *Newsweek*, March 29
1983	"OIL PRICES HIT THE SKIDS," *Newsweek*, January 24

These headlines indicate that over the period 1972–1983 Americans' attitudes concerning energy ran full cycle—from optimism (or even indifference) to panic and then back to guarded optimism.

Perhaps even more than headlines, editorial cartoons may be viewed as a reflection of prevailing public opinion. Here again we see a massive change in public opinion from 1973 to 1983. For example, in 1973, an Arabian sheik holds up a U.S. consumer with a gasoline-nozzle pistol. But in 1983, the OPEC sheiks were depicted in a far less menacing manner.

How can such a radical shift in public opinion be explained? The explanation is found in the energy market itself. Something happened to negate the forecasts of gloom and doom that were being widely publicized in the mid-1970s. In this chapter, we will review the events of the last several decades in order to identify the factors that eliminated the crisis in the energy market. (Once we finish our history of the last decade, it might be useful to return to the headlines we have

Courtesy of Mike Peters

Courtesy of Hugh Haynie

presented to see how they look in the light of the events that were occurring at the time.)

THE GOOD OLD DAYS

Before the 1970s, very few people were interested in energy except in finding more ways to use it—bigger cars, bigger houses, and so forth. It got very little attention in the press, with the possible exception of some stories about the behavior of Texas oil millionaires. Why? The answer is very simple. Before the decade of the 1970s— indeed, before 1973—the real price (price net of inflation) of oil was declining. (We definitely look back with fondness on the gas wars of the 1960s.) Let's look at the history of oil prices in the United States and in the world market for the period 1950–1970. Table 1 lists the prices for a barrel of crude oil that prevailed during this period.

It's very easy to see two major features in this price series. First, oil prices in the United States rose very little from 1950 to 1970. Second, the world price of oil stayed much below the U.S. price through 1970 and was actually falling.

These prices, however, do not take into account the effect of inflation during this period—the value of a dollar was certainly less in 1970 than it was in 1950. Hence we need to deflate these prices by a consumer price index in order to express all prices in constant dollars.

TABLE I   CRUDE OIL PRICES, 1950–1970

	Average U.S. Wellhead Price (dollars per barrel)	World Price Estimated Actual Transaction Price (dollars per barrel)
1950	$2.51	$1.71
1955	2.77	1.63
1960	2.88	1.53
1965	2.86	1.33
1970	3.18	1.26

SOURCE: James M. Griffin and Henry B. Steele, *Energy Economics and Policy*, p. 18.

In order to compare these historical prices to the prices that we are currently experiencing, we will express all of them in 1982 dollars. For those not familiar with this technique, let us explain briefly how it is done. From the published consumer price index, we know that a good that sold for $1 in 1950 sold for $4 in 1982—a 1950 dollar was worth four times as much as a dollar in 1982. Thus, a barrel of crude oil that sold for $2.51 in 1950 would carry a price tag of $10.04 in 1982. Doing the same thing for each of the prices in Table 1, we obtain the real prices of crude oil in constant 1982 dollars. We have graphed these real prices in Figure 1.

It is evident from this figure that the real price of oil fell between 1950 and the early 1970s. Is it surprising then that the 1950s and 1960s were the era of the gas guzzler in America? Is it shocking that homes built during this period were poorly insulated and energy inefficient? Of course not. If any product becomes cheaper, don't people use more of it? Don't you? Gasoline and heating oil are not exceptions. As the price of oil—and thus gasoline—dropped, cars got bigger. It wasn't a plot by the big three car manufacturers. We wanted big cars because gasoline was cheap. Efficient home energy was a rarity. Why spend a lot of money for expensive home insulation when heating oil was so cheap?

Americans weren't wasteful during this period, in spite of the editorial criticism we heard after prices rose in the 1970s. People used

FIGURE 1   CRUDE OIL PRICES, 1950–1970
(in constant 1982 dollars)

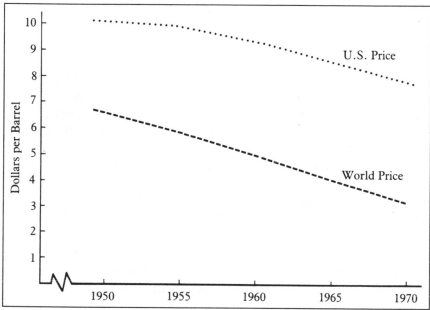

SOURCE: J.M. Griffin and H.B. Steele, *Energy Economics and Policy*, p. 18.

more of the cheap resource, oil, to save on the expensive resources—time, in the case of automobiles, and building materials, in the case of homes. This reaction is precisely what we would expect.

But during these happy days of the 1950s and 1960s, some of the seeds of the coming crisis were planted. As shown in Table 1, the world price of energy—the price of imported oil—was far below the U.S. price. So, during this period the United States began to actively follow a policy of restricting imports in order to protect domestic producers from cheap foreign crude. Ostensibly designed for national security, an oil import quota system was put in place in 1959 during the Eisenhower administration. The objective of the quota system was to limit imports to 12 percent of total U.S. consumption.

Faced with this quota system in the United States, the countries exporting that cheap crude reacted. On September 14, 1960, Iran, Iraq, Kuwait, Saudi Arabia, and Venezuela formed the Organization of Petroleum Exporting Countries (OPEC). In later years, the membership would rise to thirteen with the addition of Qatar, Indonesia, Libya, Abu Dhabi, Nigeria, Ecuador, and Gabon. However, in the 1960s, OPEC lacked the strength to become an effective cartel. The United States was producing too much oil.

Looking back at the 1960s, we can see that there was no real problem. Although OPEC existed, the demand for imported crude was insufficient for OPEC to exercise any real monopoly power. During the 1960s, there was even excess production capacity in the United States. Had OPEC attempted to reduce imports, the shortfall could easily have been covered by domestic production. What then swung the balance of power to the foreign suppliers?

Imports did not maintain a 12 percent share of U.S. consumption. The import restrictions did not work. Instead, in the 1960s, the share was closer to 20 percent. Foreign crudes were very attractive. One reason the foreign crudes were so attractive—other than the obvious reason that they were lower priced—is that many of them are low-sulfur crudes and are therefore cleaner burning. With the increasing environmental concerns of the 1960s, these clean-burning crudes became more and more desirable. And, with increasing use of these crudes, many people began to argue, quite convincingly, that elimination of import quotas would be a bonanza—it would apparently both clean up the environment and benefit consumers with lower prices. Thus, the demand for foreign crude oils increased substantially.

While this increase in the demand for foreign crude oils may have been troublesome by permitting OPEC more power, it would not have in itself led to a crisis. Instead, we would expect it to lead to higher world oil prices, although still below the U.S. price, resulting in U.S. crude becoming relatively more attractive. Rather, it was another factor that set the stage for the crisis. This factor was the price ceiling imposed on domestically produced petroleum.

A DECADE OF PANIC

In contrast to the falling real oil prices that we had experienced in the past, the decade of the 1970s was one that will be remembered for the massive increases in oil prices—particularly the price of imported oil. It was a decade of panic. Before we begin our explanation of the events of this period, let's take a moment to look at the magnitude of this increase in price. In 1970, the average cost per barrel for imported crude oil was $2.16. In 1980, it was $30.60. In order to account for the inflation that we were also experiencing during this period, it is again necessary to express these prices in constant dollars. In 1982 dollars, these values are $5.35 and $35.69, respectively. Over the eleven years from 1970 to 1980, the price of imported oil rose by over 500 percent! Figure 2 graphs the path of real price over this period. Who was responsible? Unfortunately, it turns out that we ourselves were responsible. Let us explain why.

In August 1971, the Nixon administration imposed a wage and

FIGURE 2   COST OF IMPORTED OIL, 1970–1980
(in constant 1982 dollars)

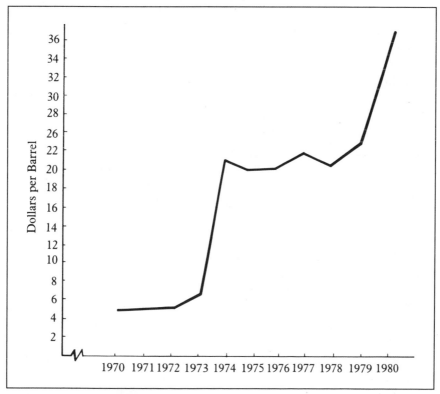

SOURCE: American Petroleum Institute, *Basic Petroleum Data Book*, January 1983.

price freeze. Think for a moment how this price ceiling affected the market for crude oil. Look first at domestic supplies. In order to obtain more energy, producers were being forced to use more and more expensive techniques—deeper wells, fracturing, steam or water injection, and so on. However, these more expensive techniques required that the producers get a higher price for the crude. Put yourself in their shoes for a moment. How long would you go on spending more and more to extract oil for which you could not charge a higher price? It is therefore not at all surprising that the peak of U.S. oil production had occurred in 1970 before the imposition of controls (at 9.6 million barrels a day). With the imposition of price controls, domestic production began its decline—a decline that would haunt us in coming years.

Next, let's look at the impact of the price ceiling on the consumption of petroleum. With declining production, consumption would also have to decline in order to avoid a shortage. Instead, consumption continued to increase at the same rate as during the oil-rush decade of the 1960s. The price controls kept the price of gasoline and heating oil from rising, so Americans continued to use oil as if nothing had happened.

By this time, the storm clouds were looming. The United States was faced with rising consumption and declining production. (Indeed, it is precisely this realization that led many to predict a collapse of the developed economies, a point we will take up later.) How then did Americans react to this situation? They imported more crude oil. By 1973, imports were approaching 30 percent of U.S. consumption. In the summer of 1973, the price controls on other products were allowed to expire; but oil was an exception. With the existing trends in consumption and production, it was clear that decontrol would lead to an increase in price; so the controls were extended through 1975 (and later until 1981). In order to avoid the price increase dictated by the market, this decision set the stage for the winter of 1973.

What was OPEC doing during the early 1970s? In 1969, the rich but feeble Libyan monarchy had been overthrown by Arab radicals led by Col. Muammar Qaddafi. This political event marked the turning point in OPEC's position. Although Libya was the smallest member of OPEC in population and GNP, its leadership excelled in fanaticism. Led by Libya, OPEC forced through a 21 percent price increase in 1971 and agreed to a program that would have amounted to a 52 percent increase (over the 1970 level) by 1976. OPEC was beginning to flex its muscles.

It was, however, in the winter of 1973 that OPEC discovered the extent of its power. As a result of the Arab-Israeli War, OPEC imposed an embargo in October. At that time, the posted price of Persian Gulf crude oils was $3.01. By the end of the year, that price had risen to $11.65—an increase of almost 300 percent in only ten weeks! (So much for OPEC's 1971 goal of a 52 percent increase over five years.) Although the embargo ended in March 1974, the remainder of the decade was one of gas lines, heating oil shortages, and OPEC price increases.

Faced with this crisis situation, how then did we, or more correctly our government, react? The obvious solution was to increase domestic production and decrease consumption. In 1975, President Gerald Ford presented a program that would have accomplished this. He proposed abolishing price controls on crude oil and imposing a $2 per barrel tax on foreign oil. Decontrol would have stimulated domestic production, while the tax would have led to a reduction in the consumption of imported oil. Instead, in 1975, Congress voted to continue the price controls. Moreover, in 1976, the governmentally-determined price of domestic crude oil was actually lowered—further reducing the incentives for domestic production.

How did we, the consumers, respond? During the embargo and immediately following, there was a massive movement toward energy efficiency. Small, fuel efficient automobiles were being sold at a substantial premium, while the large gas guzzlers sat on the lots. Home-owners began to insulate their homes and tried to reduce their use of oil and electricity. However, once the memory of the embargo faded, the conservation movement lost its momentum. With the government artificially holding down the prices the consumer had to pay, Americans returned to big cars, and it was then the small cars that were left on the used car lots. Gasoline consumption resumed its climb; indeed, consumption in 1978 was even higher than the pre-embargo record. Why did gasoline consumption remain so high in the period between 1975 and 1978? Due to price controls on petroleum, the real price of gasoline actually fell during this period. Figure 3 graphs the real prices of unleaded gasoline (in 1982 dollars) for 1970–1978. The embargo did raise the gasoline price in 1973–74; but, following this increase, the real price that consumers paid again began to decline. Price con-

FIGURE 3   UNLEADED GASOLINE PRICE, 1970–1978
                (in constant 1982 dollars)

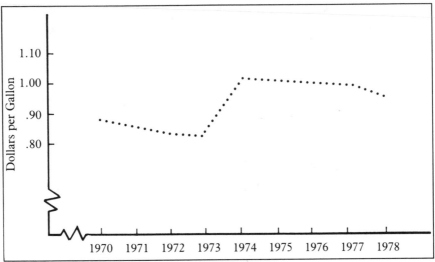

SOURCE: American Petroleum Institute, *Basic Petroleum Data Book*, January 1983.

trols insulated the consumers; so what reason existed for them to conserve gasoline?

Why then were there no gasoline lines between 1975 and 1979? The answer is simple. We imported more and more foreign crude oil. With domestic production stagnating under price controls, imports rose to almost 50 percent of total U.S. consumption.

To give more perspective on the situation that existed in the late 1970s, we have graphed consumption and production of petroleum in the United States from 1950 to 1977 in Figure 4. The imposition of price controls in 1971 led to a decline in domestic production. But these same price controls insulated consumers from the higher world price. With the exception of the temporary decline in consumption that followed the 1973 embargo, consumption continued to increase. As we neared the end of the 1970s, the gap between domestic consumption and production was getting wider and wider. The price controls begun in 1971 had set us up for the events that were to come in 1979.

The turmoil in Iran in 1979 marked the beginning of the second period of severe gasoline shortage. However, all this really did was to indicate the level of our dependence on imports. With the cutbacks in foreign production and the resultant increases in the price of crude oil, Americans experienced once again the depths of a crisis. The worst of the energy crisis was upon us; a solution to the problem became essential.

THE DOOM MERCHANTS

In light of the events that occurred during the 1970s, it is not surprising that some people predicted the imminent collapse of the world as we know it due to shortages in energy and other natural resources. When faced with a period of scarcity, there are always those who will argue that the shortages will only get worse, leading finally to

FIGURE 4   U.S. PETROLEUM CONSUMPTION AND PRODUCTION, 1950–1977

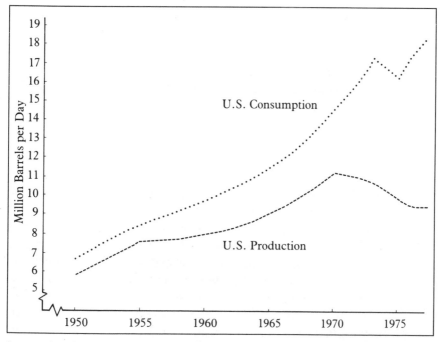

SOURCE: American Petroleum Institute, *Basic Petroleum Data Book*, January 1983.

DOOM. Looking at figures like the one we presented above, the doom merchants predicted that we are going to run out of oil. Indeed, if we were to look only at such a figure, it is not hard to see how they came to such a conclusion. But the important thing is that such a figure does not tell the whole story.

While we will concentrate on the more recent prophecies of doom in the energy market, we should note that this was not the first time experts had predicted that the world would run out of petroleum. Let us give you a few examples:

1891   The U.S. Geological Survey predicted that there was little or no chance of finding oil in Texas.

1926   The Federal Oil Conservation Board predicted the United States had only a seven-year supply of petroleum remaining. Senator LaFollette predicted that the price of gasoline would soon rise to $1 per gallon.

1939   The Interior Department predicted that U.S. petroleum supplies would last for less than two decades.

1949   The Secretary of the Interior predicted that the end to U.S. supplies of oil was almost in sight.

There were many doomsday theses advanced during the 1970s. Probably the best known is that in *The Limits to Growth* by Donella H. Meadows et al. Permit us to concentrate on the authors' argument as an illustration of the arguments proposed by the group we label the "doom merchants."

They argued that there were five prevailing trends in the world: (1) accelerating industrialization, (2) rapid population growth, (3) widespread malnutrition, (4) depletion of nonrenewable resources, and (5) deteriorating environment.

Furthermore, they asserted that in general these prevailing trends are characterized by exponential growth. Viewing these prevailing trends, the authors then made their crucial assumption: They assumed that the prevailing trends would continue in the future. Put another way, their forecasts for future levels of consumption and production were simply extrapolations from the existing trend lines. Although they argued that "extrapolation is a time-honored way of looking into the future," we will demonstrate that it certainly did not prove valid for energy. In Chapter 2, we will confront this questionable assumption more directly.

Given their assumption of prevailing trend, Meadows et al. proceeded to make some dismal forecasts for the future. They asserted that "industrial growth will certainly stop within the next century, at the latest." The limits to growth will, in their scenario, be reached within 100 years and the result will be a sudden and uncontrollable decline in both population and industrial capacity. In their view, "the basic behavior mode of the world system is exponential growth of population and capital, followed by collapse." The forecast was, then, that the future holds "a dismal, depleted existence" because of resource shortages.

What about technological progress? Can't we avert the collapse through technological advancement? Not according to these prophets of doom. They asserted that "the application of technology to apparent problems of resource depletion . . . has no impact on the *essential* problem, which is exponential growth." In essence, this statement again asserts that the prevailing trends in production and consumption will continue unchanged—technological progress cannot alter these trends.

What then was their solution? Only one solution was offered—"deliberate checks on growth." In this dismal view of the future, it was argued that we can only avert the inevitable collapse by learning to live with less. And advocates of this policy were not in short supply.

As will be demonstrated in the following sections, recent history does not bear out these dire predictions. Why not? The answer is very simple. The trends in consumption and production have changed. In the case of energy, the rate of growth in consumption declined while that for production increased. What caused these changes in trend? In their analysis, Meadows et al. neglected one crucial point—the impact of price in a marketplace. They understood that shortages lead to increases in price: "Given present resource consumption rates and the projected increase in these rates, the great majority of the currently important nonrenewable resources will be extremely costly 100 years from now." However, they failed to realize that price influences prevailing trends. For example, the trend they observed in consumption was due, to a large extent, to falling resource prices (especially energy) in the 1960s and early 1970s. However, how do consumers react if the price increases? Obviously, they consume less; so with rising prices, the

rate of increase in consumption declines. With rising prices, the users of
a resource begin to conserve it. Thus, our assertion is that these doom
merchants failed to consider the impact of price on trends. In the
following sections, we will demonstrate this point in the case of energy
and we will return to a general consideration of this issue in Chapter 2.

THE SOLUTION TO THE ENERGY CRISIS

We left our discussion of the events of the last decade in
1979—the depth of the energy crisis. At the time, it appeared to many
Americans that the problem might never be solved—that the doom
merchants might have been correct. This pessimistic attitude is probably best reflected in the headline that appeared on the cover of *Newsweek* on November 19, 1973:

"ARE WE RUNNING OUT OF EVERYTHING?"

How gloomy can you get? But happily this was an instance in which it
was indeed darkest before the dawn. The shortages of 1979 forced us
to realize that price controls were a self-defeating strategy. There was
no quick fix; no painless solution. The energy problem could not be
wished away or legislated away; it had to be faced. In the midst of a
storm of angry protest from consumer groups, President Jimmy
Carter announced that, beginning in late 1979, oil price controls
would be phased out with final decontrol occurring in the fall of 1981.

By the end of 1980, imports had fallen by 25 percent. Both consumers and producers saw that, once again, the price of energy was to
be controlled by supply and demand—not by government fiat. Consumers realized that the era of artificially cheap energy was over, so
they began to conserve energy. The important point to realize here is
that this was not just a panic reaction to short-term shortages and
gasoline lines—like the winter of 1973—but rather was a reaction to
the realization that more and more oil could be obtained only at higher
and higher prices. Faced with this realization, Americans began to
conserve gasoline and other petroleum products.

It is, however, on the production side that the impact of deregulation was most pronounced. As we have noted earlier, over time it has
become more difficult and more expensive to find and extract new

supplies of crude oil. In 1970, the average cost of drilling an onshore well was about $15 per foot. By 1980, this cost had risen to $60 per foot. Higher prices were needed to induce suppliers to find and extract new deposits of crude oil. And that is precisely what decontrol did. The rising price of crude oil made it feasible to drill deeper, use more expensive recovery techniques, and generally undertake more risky projects. Examples of the exotic new technologies include infrared photographs taken from satellites to find promising exploration sites and horizontal drilling that permits wheel spoke patterns from an original hole to drain the oil more completely from a given area.

Deregulation was completed by President Ronald Reagan in January 1981—nine months earlier than planned. What happened then? By the end of the year, consumption had dropped by 20 percent. On the other side of the coin, the drilling for new sources had increased by 50 percent. Indeed, in 1981, the number of oil rigs working in the United States was almost double that in 1979; and, not surprisingly, this number is approximately six times the number of rigs working in 1971. The result was that, for the first time in more than a decade, petroleum reserves in the United States rose. Within a month following decontrol, the price of gasoline had risen about 10 cents per gallon, with heating oil increasing by about the same amount. The price of domestic crude oil jumped from $29 to $36 per barrel, a rise that indicated a forthcoming increase in the price of gasoline of another 14 cents. However, by March the oil companies found themselves in a situation that was unusual given their experience of the past decade—a surplus of oil products at the existing prices. They reacted as any market reacts; the major oil companies cut the price of oil products. By the summer of 1981, consumers were faced with a happy situation, falling energy prices.

By the end of 1982, the ability of a functioning marketplace to eliminate a shortage had become even more evident. As shown in Figure 5, domestic consumption of petroleum had dropped radically while U.S. production continued to increase. The gap between domestic consumption and production had declined to its precontrol magnitude. Imports were at the lowest level in eleven years. As Figure 6 illustrates, imports as a percentage of total U.S. demand have dropped steadily since decontrol. The workings of a marketplace have broken the stranglehold OPEC held on America!

What about OPEC? With decontrol, America and other Western

FIGURE 5   U.S. PETROLEUM CONSUMPTION AND PRODUCTION,
              1970–1982

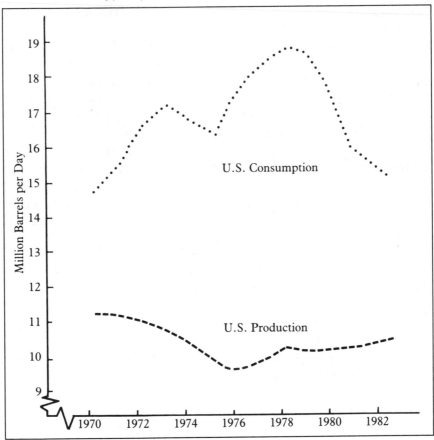

SOURCES: American Petroleum Institute, *Basic Petroleum Data Book*, January 1983; U.S. Department of Energy, *Monthly Energy Review*, January 1983.

countries became less dependent on OPEC oil. In 1973, OPEC accounted for almost 60 percent of the oil supply of the West, but by 1982 this share had fallen below 45 percent. In 1981 and, most particularly, in 1982, OPEC was producing more high priced oil than the world wanted. In an effort to maintain its price, OPEC members—led by Saudi Arabia—tried to reduce production. But this move met with little success. Iran, for one, increased its production sixfold—from one half million to over three million barrels per day—in only the last six months of 1982. The world was virtually awash in oil. In 1982, we saw something we had not seen for a long time—a decline in the price of imported oil. According to the U.S. Department of Energy, the average acquisition cost of a barrel of imported crude oil fell from $37.05 in 1981 to $33.72 in 1982. Even more significantly, we began to read about "the end of OPEC." Permit us to show you two of the headlines appearing in early 1983.

> "OPEC OUTPUT PACT COLLAPSES"
> *Washington Post*, January 28, 1983

> "OPEC: FROM CARTEL TO CHAOS"
> *Newsweek*, March 7, 1983

While it may be a little too early for us to write the final obituary for OPEC, it is clear that the energy crisis we suffered through in the 1970s is over. OPEC will probably continue to exist, but it does not today and will not in the future have the power it had during the 1970s (unless we again hand it that power). By allowing the market to function, we survived the energy crisis.

FIGURE 6   IMPORTS AS A PERCENTAGE OF TOTAL U.S. DEMAND, 1950–1982

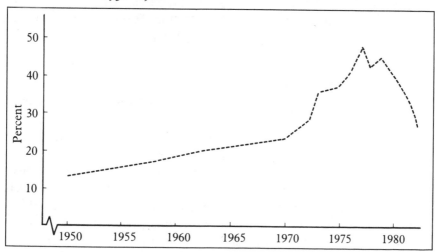

SOURCES: American Petroleum Institute, *Basic Petroleum Data Book*, January 1983; U.S. Department of Energy, *Monthly Energy Review*, January 1983.

THE MORAL

In *Poor Richard's Almanac*, Benjamin Franklin said something about experience keeping a hard school. Since we have all had to suffer through the harsh experience of this recent energy crisis, we need to make sure we have learned the lessons it taught. Permit us to summarize what we feel are the most important of these lessons as the answers to three questions.

What caused the crisis?   As Richard Hofstadter has pointed out, Americans have formed conspiracy theories before. At various times, the conspirators have been the Masons, Catholics, slaveholders, international bankers, munitions manufacturers, and the House of Hapsburg. During the decade of the 1970s, many persons again turned to a conspiracy theory in which OPEC and the oil companies were the villains. (Indeed, a reader of *Science Digest* noted to the editors the diabolical fact that OPEC had thirteen members; and we all know about the dark forces involved in the number thirteen.) However, although OPEC raised the price of oil and the oil companies charged us higher prices, the truth is that we ourselves, not some outside agent, caused the crisis. Instead of permitting the marketplace to function, we, through our agents the government, attempted to keep the price of oil artificially low. In doing so, we caused consumption to increase and domestic production to decline. With this growing gap between domestic consumption and production, we placed ourselves at the mercy of foreign suppliers.

What about the forecasts of doom for the developed economies?   Those who predicted doom did so on the basis of trends prevailing at that time. They saw that the rate of growth in consumption exceeded the rate of growth for production. Obviously, if that trend continued, we would run out of oil. However, those trends changed. Once price was permitted to rise, the rate of growth in consumption declined while the rate of growth of production increased. Look at Figure 5. The upshot of this is that in the 1980s we find ourselves not faced by a shortage of oil but rather with the happy circumstance of falling prices. The doom merchants neglected a critical variable—price. In a market economy, a shortage leads to an increase in price, which always has and always will result in a decline in consumption and an increase in production.

What eliminated the crisis?   Here the answer is very simple; our market economy eliminated the energy crisis of the 1970s. Once the price mechanism was permitted to function—after a delay of ten years—the gap between domestic consumption and production began to narrow rapidly. With increasing energy prices, consumption declined. Conservation was accomplished by the consumers substituting other commodities for the relatively expensive energy. We substituted newer, more fuel efficient autos for those of an earlier decade. In 1973, the average auto in the United States obtained 13.1 miles per gallon. By 1981 the average miles per gallon for autos in the United States was 15.5. The fuel efficiency of U.S. autos has increased by over 18 percent. In our homes, we substituted insulation (and sometimes sweaters) for energy. Firms also substituted capital for energy by switching from inefficient machines to more energy efficient machines. Hence, we argue that one of the primary factors is the price-induced substitution away from energy. Looking at the production of oil, we saw that rising oil prices led to a massive increase in domestic exploration and drilling. The resulting increase in production can, to a great extent, be said to involve price-induced technical change. As prices rose, the producers were induced to use newer and more expensive technology in order to drill deeper, drill in more difficult formations and locations, and extract more of the available deposit. With the new technology, oil fields that were previously not counted as reserves began pumping oil. Therefore, we feel that price-induced substitution and price-induced technical change are responsible for solving the energy crisis.

We might ask the question, "Was it a miracle?" Well, if one remembers those long gas lines back in 1979, the answer is "yes." How else could so serious a problem go away in such a short period of time? And we would probably have to agree. Sometimes the results of freely functioning markets seem like a miracle. No one person, no government, no regulatory body was needed to solve the crisis. The real miracle was that individual consumers and producers, acting independently in their own self-interest, eliminated the crisis by responding to price changes.

We might also ask, "Was it unprecedented?" To this question we answer, "no." As we shall show, this miracle had occurred many times before. Crises that were thought to be insurmountable were overcome in the same way that the energy crisis was solved. This then is the theme of our book: these miracles have happened in the past, and there is no reason to believe that they won't continue to happen in the future.

IS THE ENERGY CRISIS *REALLY* OVER?

At this time, imports have declined from almost 50 percent to less than 30 percent of domestic consumption. To that extent, we no longer have to fear upheavals caused by a curtailment of foreign oil, like those of 1973 or 1979. Hence, the energy crisis in the sense of massive shortages is over.

On a larger scale, an energy crisis still may exist. It is getting harder and more expensive to find and extract crude oil. In a free market, this means that the future might hold higher prices for energy products. While we are sure the world will never run out of oil, it is possible that sometime in the future oil may become so expensive that it is no longer feasible to use it as an energy source. What then? Permit us to hold the answer to this question for a later chapter. Once we have seen what has happened in the past, we will be in a much better position to answer that question.

THE
DISMAL
SCIENCE

2

IN the preceding chapter, we examined the energy crisis of the 1970s. Based on the trends in consumption and production that prevailed in the earlier part of the decade, many writers went so far as to predict the collapse of the developed economies due to resource shortages. We heard people talking about the day "when the pumps run dry." Over and over, the physical scientists pointed to entropy—the second law of thermodynamics—as clear and definitive proof that we were going to run out of oil. (In the context of the energy crisis, the entropy law would say something like "deposits of petroleum are finite and you can't burn the same barrel of petroleum twice.") The shortcoming of their analysis was that they presupposed that the trends in consumption and production that prevailed in the early 1970s would continue into the future. They neglected the impact that prices have on consumers and producers. While these merchants of doom agreed that the shortage would raise the price of gasoline and other petroleum products, they did not recognize that changes in price will change the behavior of participants in a marketplace.

In fact, the rapid increases in the price of energy altered prevailing trends. As we showed in the first chapter, with rising energy prices the rate of increase in the consumption of petroleum products declined, while the rate of growth in production increased. The net result was, of course, a surplus (or, as the press called it, a glut) at existing prices rather than a shortage in the energy market by the early 1980s. The energy crisis was ended, not through repeal of the second law of thermodynamics, but rather as a result of the laws of demand and supply: as prices rise, consumers will use less and producers will bring more to the market.

This experience with energy in the 1970s provides what we feel is a very optimistic view of the future for market economies. Specifically, it implies that when an economy is faced with a shortage, price will rise, leading to reduced consumption and increased production, thereby eliminating the shortage. Doomsday will be averted. We feel that such a prediction would earn economics the label of "the optimistic science." Instead, economics is (we feel inappropriately) labeled as "the dismal science." Let us begin by taking a moment to see how this label came about.

THOMAS MALTHUS'S PREDICTIONS OF DOOM

In the latter part of the eighteenth century, a British economist, Thomas Malthus, proposed a dismal view of the future for the world that was in marked contrast to the prevailing optimism of the time. On the basis of his observations of historical trends, he argued that population grows at a geometric rate (e.g., 1, 2, 4, 8, 16, 32, . . .) while food production increases at an arithmetic rate (e.g., 1, 2, 3, 4, 5, 6, . . .). We provide a graphical interpretation of Malthus's assertion in Figure 7. As is clear from the figure, such a view implies that given prevailing rates of growth, there will come a time at which the increase in population overtakes the increase in food production; so famine is inevitable. Indeed, Malthus forecasted recurring periods of starvation, with the long-run level of consumption at only the minimum subsistence level—certainly a dismal projection. (You might be interested to know what Malthus proposed as a solution. In keeping with his beliefs as an Anglican clergyman, he opposed both contraception and abortion. Instead, he supported "moral restraint"—later marriages, cold baths, and so forth. It is also interesting to note that Malthus opposed any relief to the poor. In his view, the poor had brought the problem [excess population] on themselves; any relief measures would simply aggravate the problem.)

It is this dismal prediction (and equally dismal solution) that led to

FIGURE 7   MALTHUS'S PREDICTION OF DOOM

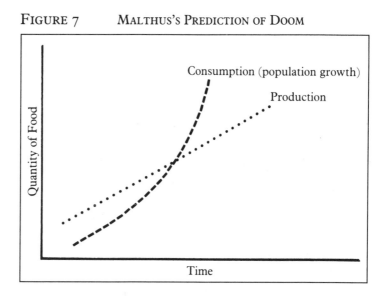

economics being labeled "the dismal science." This kind of prediction, which asserts that the growth rate in consumption will swamp the growth rate in production, is normally referred to as Malthusian. In view of such dire predictions, it is not surprising that the word "Malthusian" has taken on dreary connotations. (We find it interesting that the current doom merchants refer to themselves—or each other—as neo-Malthusians.)

However, the most important fact is that Malthus's predictions of doom did not come true. Malthus's predictions were wrong. The reason he was wrong is that the prevailing rates of growth did not continue into the future. The growth trends in population and food production changed, with the most significant change coming in the growth rate of food production. One has only to compare the methods employed in agriculture today with those of the eighteenth century to see this. Malthus's dismal predictions were negated by technological change. The market responded to the increased demand for food (i.e., the increase in population) and the corresponding increase in price with technological improvements in food production. (To be fair, we must note that in later years Malthus himself became more optimistic. His subsequent publications recognized the importance of technological change and opened the possibility that the prevailing trends could change. Indeed, we might say that in his later years Malthus was not a "Malthusian.")

Some 150 years after the population doomsdayers of the Malthus era, many economists were guilty of forecasting, again incorrectly as it turned out, a population problem of another sort. This time the predicted crisis was underpopulation rather than too rapid growth; but once again the doomsday prophets made the same mistake of extrapolating from past trends.

During the great depression of the 1930s, the birth rate fell dramatically in the United States and other Western countries. The reason for the decline was, of course, the massive depression. After World War II, many economists predicted continued depression. So sure were the prophets that the slump would continue indefinitely, that they coined the term "secular stagnation."

The reason for expecting secular stagnation was the projected decline in population predicted from continued decreases in the birth rate. These predictions were extrapolated from the birth figures prior to and during World War II. A lower population meant a lower demand for consumer goods, and, because of the lower demand for goods, the low rate of investment and employment would continue. As soldiers became civilians again and defense industries were closed, the lack of demand would cause a huge increase in unemployment. And the unemployment would continue indefinitely. Hence, secular stagnation—a return to the depression.

But it didn't happen that way. What happened was one of the biggest population explosions ever—the postwar baby boom. Accumulated savings from the war period when incomes were high and many consumer goods were unavailable became new buying power. Newly formed families demanded houses, automobiles, appliances. All of these industries and many others needed labor. Europe had to be rebuilt. The result was high employment and investment. The forecasted secular stagnation didn't come. What came was the boom of the late 1940s and 1950s. As was the case with the earlier (over)population crisis, the underpopulation crisis just did not happen. Like Malthus, these later prophets of doom were wrong, because they based their dire predictions on previous trends. The trends simply didn't continue.

MALTHUS AND THE CURRENT DOOM MERCHANTS

When we look back on Malthus's dire forecast from the viewpoint of the late twentieth century, we often think it is simply silly to predict that trends existing at that time would continue into the future. How could Malthus have been so naive? However, the problem is that nothing has changed; people are still predicting Malthusian crises.

A clear example is found in the forecasts of doom based on energy and other natural resources that we described in the preceding chapter. Think about it for a moment. How did Meadows and the other merchants of doom come up with their predictions? They assumed that prevailing trends in consumption and production would continue in the future and that, given these trends, there will come a time when the consumption of energy (or tin, or copper, or other resources) will overtake production and a famine becomes inevitable. Doesn't that sound familiar? It is exactly the same kind of prediction that Malthus made in 1798.

Malthus was wrong. Price-induced technological change negated his dismal forecast. And, as we argued in the first chapter, we see no evidence that there is an energy famine in our future. The market responded to the oil shortage and resulting increase in price with both technological improvements and substitution, eliminating the shortage. In both of these instances—Malthus's food crisis and our own recent energy crisis—the trends in consumption and production changed; they did not remain at their historical growth rates. Why did they change? The answer is found in price, the variable that is neglected in these trend extrapolations. If a shortage of a particular product occurs, its price goes up. As the price goes up, consumers try to use less of it; so the rate of growth in consumption declines. Conversely, with rising prices, producers try to bring more to the market to sell, and the rate of growth in production increases. Furthermore, the higher price of the product induces people to search for substitutes. Technological change is induced. Putting all these forces together, we argue that if the marketplace is permitted to function, the famine (or collapse) will never come about.

To this point, we have concentrated on the forecasts of collapse in the energy market that were made in the 1970s. As you might expect, the merchants of doom looked at other markets as well. Let us give you an example. As Julian Simon pointed out, in 1969 Paul Ehrlich predicted that "the end of the ocean came in the late summer of 1979." More specifically, Ehrlich predicted that the world fish catch would decline to 30 million metric tons in 1977—in turn leading to the starvation of 50 million people per year. Instead, according to Simon, the world fish catch in 1977 was 73 million tons—more than twice what Ehrlich had predicted. Another doomsday averted.

Given that so many of their dismal predictions have been proved false, you might think the doom merchants would quit the field. Such is simply not the case. There is no shortage of those predicting doom. For example, in 1981 a program was produced for the Public Broadcasting System (PBS) by KUED (Salt Lake City) entitled "The Doomsayers." The tone of this program was set in the opening by the narrator:

> Now there are those who say that Western civilization has run its course. That our efforts to create a society of peace and prosperity have nearly failed. That ahead of us waits the prospect of a new dark age. Around us rise the voices of the doomsayers.

In this program, the doomsayers who were interviewed painted a picture of gloom and doom to gladden the hearts of the neo-Malthusians. In contrast to the optimism we want to convey to you, these doom merchants pointed to "the spectre of economic collapse." And, like many of their colleagues during the 1970s, they based much of the case for economic collapse on the prediction that we are going to run out of resources. As made explicit by David Brower, the chairman of Friends of the Earth, this prediction was again based on the idea of finite resources being consumed at an exponentially increasing rate. The impact of price on the behavior of consumers and producers was still not considered. The doom merchants continued to predict the future on the basis of trends that had existed in the past.

Another example of the current dismal predictions made by the doom merchants is found in *One Hundred Pages for the Future*, which was published in the United States in 1982, a report by Aurelio Peccei, president of the Club of Rome. (*Limits to Growth* was the first report published by the Club of Rome.) In the first paragraph of the foreword to the U.S. edition, Peccei sets the tone of his predictions: "There is no doubt in my mind that the human race is hurtling toward disaster." Although he attempts to divorce himself from extrapolative forecasting, much of the book is based upon trend forecasting (for example, his predictions for population and resource consumption). Once again, predictions are made without any consideration of the impact of price on the behavior of consumers and producers. However, Peccei clearly states why he gives no credence to the marketplace. In his opinion: "Neither the producer nor the consumer, not even society itself can any longer trust the 'invisible hand' of classical economics . . . Instead, they often find themselves kicked along by a 'mysterious boot.' " So in 1982, even after our experience with decontrol of the energy market, we find that the Club of Rome—the philosophical home of so many of the doom merchants—continues to assert that there exist "dangers that threaten our very survival" and that the marketplace has somehow stopped functioning. In order to survive, "everything must be invented anew."

It is precisely this attitude that we oppose. We hope to be able to show you that the marketplace is and can remain vital. In contrast to the opinion forwarded by the Club of Rome, the marketplace is not dead. As in the case of our recent energy crisis, it can be relied upon to eliminate shortages—crises—and thereby avert the doomsday that some assert is upon us. But before we go on, permit us to take a moment to say one or two things more about the extrapolative forecasting technique that has formed the basis for most of the predictions of gloom and doom.

THE SHOE ON THE OTHER FOOT

As is probably clear by now, we are not at all convinced by forecasts based on prevailing trend, regardless of the assertion by Meadows et al. that "extrapolation is a time-honored way of looking into the future." Experience has shown us that shortages or surpluses will change the price of the commodity, which in turn will alter the prevailing rates of growth of consumption and production. Price changes alter the trends.

To illustrate more clearly the shortcomings of trend extrapolation, let us turn it on itself. For purposes of illustration, we will call *The*

Limits to Growth (1972) the first of the (modern) doomsday books; so in 1972 a library would contain only one such book. However, the publication of *The Limits to Growth* brought many similar books to the market. In 1973, we found that six such books were published, including titles like *The Failure of Success.* Hence, in 1973, our doomsday shelf would contain seven books. The actual publication of doomsday books over the period 1972–1977 is summarized in Table 2. Note that in 1977 the doomsday shelf in our library would have contained 26 books.

From Table 2, we calculated the prevailing rate of growth of doomsday books over this period. This gave us an annual growth rate of 75 percent. Now let's forecast the number of doomsday books that will exist in the year 2000. Like Malthus and the modern doom merchants, we will assume that the prevailing trend is unchanged. Then, extrapolating from the prevailing trend, we would forecast that in the year 2000 there will exist over 14 million doomsday books! In 1983, the total holdings of the Library of Congress—books and pamphlets— was something less than 20 million items. Let us give you another way to put this number in some perspective. Visualize the library shelf holding the doomsday books. If each book were two inches thick, the shelf would be 450 miles long.

Obviously, our forecast is silly. The point is, however, that we admit it, while the doom merchants argue that theirs are somehow reliable. Theirs and ours are based on the same invalid assumption that prevailing trends will continue in the future.

TABLE 2   DOOMSDAY BOOKS PUBLISHED, 1972–1977

	Published	Cumulative Total
1972	1	1
1973	6	7
1974	2	9
1975	4	13
1976	6	19
1977	7	26

We hope you have seen our point; but we simply can not resist telling you one more story to illustrate the dangers inherent in extrapolative forecasting. On one of the late night TV programs we heard a guest provide a tongue-in-cheek forecast that went something like this: if George Steinbrenner continues to behave as he has in the past, by the year 2004, 70 percent of the male population of New York will have managed the Yankees. (Here we might suggest the alternative prediction that Billy Martin will have managed the Yankees 6,000 times.) While such a forecast is clearly farfetched, it does rest on the same assumption that is present in all extrapolative forecasts: if prevailing trends continue, then . . .

Our point is simple. We have never seen an instance where prevailing trends have continued far into the future. Conditions always change. While we are not sure what might alter George Steinbrenner's behavior in the future, we do know how prevailing trends in consumption and production have been altered in the past and will be altered in the future—the trends are altered by changes in the price of the resource.

THE MARKET WORKS

Let us take a moment to see where we stand. In the eighteenth century, Malthus predicted that a food famine was inevitable, given the prevailing trends in production and consumption. This prediction was negated because those trends changed. Specifically, technological progress in agriculture substantially increased the rate of growth of food production. In the twentieth century, many writers predicted a famine in energy and a resultant collapse of the developed economies, again given the prevailing trends in production and consumption. By the 1980s, the forecasted shortage turned into a glut of petroleum. The crisis was averted because the trends changed. As the price of energy rose, consumers used less energy. By and large, this energy saving was the result of technical improvements and the substitution of more energy efficient cars and appliances for the gas guzzlers. Also, as the price of energy rose, producers delivered more energy. Formerly expensive technology for extracting more oil became economically practical at the higher energy prices.

In both of these instances, the fact that crisis and collapse were avoided was due not to any altruistic motives on the part of consumers or producers nor to the intervention of a forward-looking and benevolent government but rather to the actions of a freely functioning marketplace. The working of the market is simplicity itself. If something becomes more scarce, its price rises. As the price rises, consumers try to use less of it. How do they do so? They can either rely on technological change that makes the scarce good less essential or substitute some other commodity for the scarce good. As the price of the scarce commodity rises, producers try to provide more of it to the market. How can this be accomplished? Producers can either use new technology to provide more of the commodity in question or they can begin supplying a substitute for the scarce commodity. The end result is that, with reduced consumption and increased production, the shortage is eliminated and the price of the commodity will begin to fall.

Our thesis is very simple—we argue that markets work to eliminate shortages; so forecasts of doom or collapse based on shortages are groundless. The "invisible hand" (as first described by Adam Smith in *The Wealth of Nations*) is not palsied, as the president of the Club of Rome asserted. To paraphrase Mark Twain's famous cable to the Associated Press, we believe that the reports of the death of the marketplace are greatly exaggerated. If a shortage occurs, price will increase and the price increase will adjust consumption and production so as to eliminate the shortage. We feel that there are two major mechanisms by which this adjustment is accomplished—substitution and price-induced technological change. As price rises, consumers substitute some other commodity for the scarce commodity. During the energy crisis, didn't you or your acquaintances substitute some insulation for the scarce—and more expensive—fuel oil? As prices rise, individuals are induced to undertake technological innovation that will reduce consumption of the scarce commodity or replace it entirely. What brought about more efficient automobile engines and air conditioning systems in the late 1970s? Under what conditions would you consider heating or cooling your house using some alternate technology like solar power?

So far, we have described two instances in which the free market has worked its "miracle"—the recent energy crisis and Malthus's food crisis. We wondered if there were other instances in which a free market had averted a crisis due either to prevailing trends in consumption and production or to some outside curtailment of supplies. We started to look for examples in which technological progress and/or substitution eliminated what were apparently very critical shortages. We were simply amazed at the number of these instances. In the next seven chapters, we will recount some of these stories.

AN
EARLIER
"CRUDE"
CRISIS

3

DURING the early days of World War II, the United States experienced a natural resource crisis that was much more serious than the crude oil crisis of the 1970s. The crisis involved crude rubber, rather than crude oil. America and its allies imported an extremely large proportion of the rubber they consumed from the Far East—in 1940 all but 2 percent of U.S. rubber consumption came from Far Eastern countries. And these same rubber supplying countries were rapidly conquered by the Japanese in 1941 and early 1942. There was practically no natural rubber anywhere else in the world. So the United States was fighting a major war on two fronts while the enemy controlled the entire supply of a resource that was indispensable in modern warfare. Now that's a crisis!

The fact that this rubber crisis was so quickly—almost miraculously—solved by the development of synthetic rubber has led to what we call an American fable. Instead of us telling you this fable ourselves, permit us to relate a version of it that was told by a prominent U.S. congressman in 1979. For reasons that will become clear later, the congressman will remain anonymous.

> The President [Franklin Roosevelt] had become increasingly concerned that our supplies of the critically important commodity could be interrupted by hostility toward the United States in the area of the world that supplied most of our imports. He knew that

imports from allies and other stable sources would not be sufficient to offset the effect of a massive interruption of imports from
our major suppliers of the commodity. The President's conviction
that the United States must move quickly to develop a substitute
for the commodity was shared by his advisers and Congressional
leaders.

Despite some opposition, Congress passed the legislation necessary to begin the effort to develop a synthetic substitute. As
expected, our imports were cut off. But within two years of the
interruption of imports, using the skills and technology of American business, the United States had developed a new industry to
produce a synthetic substitute. And not only could we produce
enough of the substitute to replace a substantial portion of lost
imports—the synthetic proved to be better and cheaper than the
commodity it replaced.

The congressman related this fable to justify a national synthetic
fuel program. Others used, and are still using, this fable about the
development of synthetic rubber to argue for a huge government
program to develop alternative energy sources. On the face of it,
this sounds great; but there's just one problem: the fable is dead
wrong!

It is certainly true that within months of the entry of the United
States into the war the Japanese had cut off the entire supply of
natural rubber to the United States and Great Britain. It is also true
that by the end of the war American industry was producing huge
amounts of synthetic rubber—practically all of the war requirements
of the United States and England with some left over for civilian
consumption. However, it is not true that synthetic rubber began
from scratch in 1941 and resulted from a massive government development program. The fact is that the technology necessary for the
manufacture of synthetic rubber had already been developed before
America's entry into the war. The headlines from an article in the
August 1940 issue of *Fortune* (over a year before Pearl Harbor was
bombed) tell the story.

SYNTHETIC RUBBER

If War Cuts Our 600,000-Ton Rubber Life Line to the Far East,
the Neoprenes and Bunas and Butyles Are Ready in Prepared
Positions. They Are Building a New Industry in Any Event.

ON THE U.S. FRONTIER
Synthetic Rubber Is Teetering on the Edge of a Blazing New
Frontier—a War Frontier in Which It May Be Called upon to
Man the Stockades. It Is Ready.

Obviously, the synthetic rubber industry was ready and waiting
when the natural rubber supply was cut off by the Japanese army. But
why did it exist? Some hints are found in the last paragraph of that
story in *Fortune:*

> In whatever way synthetic rubber goes, it is a portent of "the
> changed world" ahead. Price is the critical lever. Raw materials
> for synthetic rubbers are cheap in the United States, labor in
> semiautomatic chemical processes is negligible—small volume has
> been the stumbling block. But there are signs that that block is
> soon to be kicked. For Standard Oil is big—big volume and
> small-profit minded—and Standard has a hunch that synthetic-
> rubber prices can be brought down to natural rubber. Against the
> cost of maintaining a 12,000-mile supply line and inventories at
> the mercy of the rubber cartel, the industry is beginning to view a
> steady, domestic source for rubber as a new imperative. This kind
> of natural self-sufficiency is on the way. It is a remaker of maps
> more powerful than Hitler.

A "rubber cartel?" The American rubber fable the congressman
told us didn't mention anything about a cartel. It looks as though an
examination of the history of the rubber industry might be in order.

THE FIRST RUBBER CRISIS, 1895–1910

The first rubber crisis in the United States took place
around the turn of the century when the price of crude rubber,
gathered from trees growing wild in Africa and Latin America (particularly Brazil), took a tremendous leap. In the late 1890s, the price
of rubber more than doubled, from around 50 cents to over $1.00 a
pound. The price of natural rubber continued to rise, reaching a peak
of $3.06 a pound in 1910, a six-fold increase in a little over ten years.
Then the trend reversed; the price fell to 20 cents a pound over the
next ten years. What happened?

Well, in the first place, the rapid development of the automobile industry after the turn of the century, particularly in the United States, substantially increased the demand for tires and tubes, driving up the price of rubber. As always, the rapidly rising price induced more and more production. In 1890, rubber trees in Latin America produced less than 20,000 tons. By 1900, over 30,000 tons were produced. The tonnage was over 40,000 in 1910, and the real expansion in automobile production was just beginning.

But because no one owned the rubber trees, no one had any incentive to conserve them. The forests were free to anyone. Sap was collected from rubber trees in the fastest way possible—by chopping them down. If one producer, wishing to conserve trees, extracted sap by milking them, someone else would come along and cut the trees down. So what was the point in anyone conserving? For this reason, the great rubber forests were destroyed, pushing the price of raw rubber even higher. Extraction from trees in Mexico and the Congo was increased, but not enough to hold down prices.

The tremendous increase in the price of rubber had two important consequences—one legal; the other, not so legal. Years before, Brazil and other countries with rubber trees passed laws against taking cuttings of plantings of rubber trees out of the country. This was rational. Certainly, if a country has a virtual monopoly of an important commodity, it wants to keep that monopoly for itself. But when that commodity becomes incredibly profitable, there is a tremendous incentive for other producers to get in on the action. Sure enough, some enterprising entrepreneurs did smuggle plantings out of Brazil and took them to the Far East, specifically to the British and Dutch colonies where the climate and growing conditions were similar to those in Brazil. Conditions in that region proved favorable and the great rubber plantations of the Far East were begun.

In 1900, 4 tons were produced by these plantations. By 1910, production rose to a higher, but still meager, 8,000 tons. In five more years, output from the Far East, chiefly Malaya, reached an astounding 95,000 tons. The rest of the world, including Brazil, produced only 40,000 tons. The plantation system had, in effect, replaced wild rubber. Not surprisingly, with so much additional crude rubber available, the price of rubber was affected. It fell to around 50 cents a pound and continued to fall until 1922. Gathering wild rubber as a method of production was killed by its own inefficiency and replaced

by a more efficient system. By 1922, over 400,000 tons were exported
from the plantations in the Far East—93 percent of the total world
supply of natural rubber.

The high price of natural rubber also had a second far-reaching
effect. During the period of high rubber prices, the major rubber
companies instructed their chemists to find a way to turn discarded or
worn out rubber into usable raw rubber. The search—begun by the
Diamond Rubber Company—was successful. Most of the technical
problems were solved, and by the early 1920s the average annual
consumption of reclaimed rubber in the United States was 65,000
tons, well over 20 percent of the annual consumption of crude.
Recycled rubber was to have major implications in two future rubber
crises. In fact, reclaimed rubber was to become the major price stabil-
izer in the rubber market.

Hence, the increased demand for rubber and the destruction of
wild rubber trees led to the first rubber crisis. But, we can see that the
resulting increase in the price of rubber eliminated the crisis. With the
six-fold increase in price, both substitution (in the sense of an alternative source) and technical change (reclaimed rubber) occurred. The
new sources of rubber led to a decline in the price of rubber in the
same way that new petroleum reserves decreased our gasoline prices.

THE GREAT RUBBER CONSPIRACY, 1922–1925

With the huge expansion of the rubber plantations and the
development of reclaimed rubber, the average price of crude rubber
fell dramatically. By 1922, the price had fallen below 20 cents a
pound. To combat these falling prices, the Dutch and British adopted
a voluntary plan calling for restriction of production. This plan was in
effect from November 1920 to December 1921. The plan called for a
25 percent reduction in normal monthly rubber production in Malaya
and the Netherlands Indies. But the voluntary agreement didn't work
very well. In 1921, exports fell by only 12 percent from those in 1920,
and prices continued to fall. The plan was not renewed.

But because of depressed rubber prices and large surplus stocks of
rubber, the government of Great Britain instituted the Stevenson
Plan. This plan in effect created a cartel designed to restrict output
and drive up the price of natural rubber. The plan originated in
October 1921 when Winston Churchill, then secretary of state for the

colonies, appointed the Stevenson committee to examine the rubber situation and make recommendations. (Five of the eight members of the committee were directors of rubber companies and the chairman, Sir James Stevenson, was financially interested in the rubber industry.) The committee rejected voluntary restriction of output because of the previous failure and recommended compulsory curtailment of production. At the time, British colonies accounted for 72 percent of total rubber production. The vast majority of the remaining production came from the Netherlands Indies. The British government approved restrictions on output, but the Netherlands did not. In spite of this rejection by the Dutch, the British adopted the plan, which went into effect in November 1922.

The actual plan was extremely complicated, involving floating prices and exchanges. But the end result was a restriction of exports to 60 percent of standard—defined by using previous levels of exports. The Stevenson Plan was a pure and simple formation of a price-fixing cartel.

At first, price did not rise, because of the availability of huge stocks of rubber in the rubber consuming nations. In fact, the price of rubber actually fell slightly until 1924. By this time, however, the stockpiles were practically depleted. In the meantime, Great Britain reduced the permitted exports from 60 to 55 percent, then to 50 percent during the fall of 1924. The price of rubber began to rise dramatically.

From late 1924 to mid-1925, the price of rubber more than tripled. Rubber prices rose from below 30 cents a pound to more than a dollar. Despite protests from the United States, which consumed 75 percent of all rubber, Great Britain remained unyielding. The cartel was working. (However, given our recent experience, we do not think that many of you are surprised by that.)

But several things began happening in 1925 and 1926. First, the high price of rubber induced conservation in the United States. The rubber guzzlers began to conserve rubber. Second, the rapidly rising price brought forth huge increases in production from the Netherlands Indies. The Dutch, by adopting new technologies, were able to increase the average yield per acre from 300 or 400 pounds to 650 pounds and very soon to 1,300 pounds. This represented a dramatic increase in supply.

Finally, and very important for the future, the high price of natural rubber gave impetus to expansion of the young reclaimed rubber industry. Recall that reclaimed rubber began because of the high price of natural rubber between 1900 and 1910. In 1926 and 1927, the rubber industry greatly expanded its reclaimed rubber capacity. The industry also improved its technology both in reclaiming used rubber and in substituting reclaimed rubber for crude. About a fourth of all rubber produced during 1920–1924 was reclaimed. After increases in crude rubber prices, that portion increased to one-half by 1927.

So the market reacted to the rubber cartel and the resulting high price of rubber in three ways, and these reactions tended to drive the price back down. These forces were increased rubber conservation in the United States, increased production in the Netherlands Indies— an alternative source of supply—and the development of a strong reclaimed rubber industry—another alternative source. Furthermore, the high price encouraged new plantings, which increased total capacity substantially during the early 1930s. Price fell below 40 cents in 1927 and to slightly over 20 cents in 1928, when the Stevenson Plan was abandoned. The cartel was broken.

Doesn't this story sound familar? A cartel is formed and it increases the price of the resource. The consumers react to the high price with conservation and recycling. The high price induces other suppliers to adopt new technologies and thereby increase production. Although this discussion concerns crude rubber rather than crude oil, the story is the same.

The rubber cartel and the resulting high price of rubber led to another even more important result—the discovery of synthetic rubber. While synthetic rubber did not help break the cartel, producers in the United States and Germany were scared. Spurred by the possibility of future cartels and high prices, they began to search for a synthetic substitute for rubber so that they would not be at the mercy of a price-fixing cartel again. As we will see, this price-induced technological change was successful.

THE SEARCH FOR SYNTHETIC— THE EARLY YEARS

After the failure of the Stevenson Plan—the collapse of a cartel—the price of rubber fell dramatically. By 1931, the price was under 5 cents per pound. Because of the low price of rubber, the British, Dutch, and French in 1934 signed the International Rubber Regulation Agreement (IRRA). This agreement, although vaguely worded, represented a loose output control scheme—another cartel. And the agreement was moderately successful for the participants. The price of rubber rose from 6 cents in 1933, to 12 cents in 1934, then to slightly over 20 cents in the early part of 1937.

For various reasons, not the least of which was the existence of the rubber cartels, companies in the United States and Europe had continued searching for a substitute—synthetic rubber. In 1925, DuPont began research to discover a synthetic. They continued to search even after the Stevenson Plan was abandoned and rubber prices tumbled. The search was long but finally proved successful. By 1931, DuPont chemists had discovered a way to make a synthetic rubber, later called "neoprene."

When DuPont announced the discovery in 1931, rubber was selling at 5 cents a pound. Still, they continued construction of a factory to make synthetic rubber, spurred by the possibility that another cartel could be established. In 1932, neoprene was selling in the market at $1.05 a pound—and manufacturers bought it. In many ways, neoprene was better than natural rubber. For example, it resisted oil, gasoline, and chemicals better than natural rubber. In each year from 1931 through 1935, the sale of neoprene doubled. Over one and a half million pounds were sold during this period. Over the same period, the price of neoprene fell from $1.05 a pound to 65 cents. As we shall see, DuPont's neoprene capacity continued to increase until, at the beginning of World War II, the company had the capacity to produce synthetic rubber in very large quantities.

After the Stevenson Plan, I.G. Farben in Germany, Standard Oil of New Jersey, and several large rubber companies in the United States began research into synthetic rubber. In large part encouraged by German war plans, I.G. Farben had considerable success in developing a process to make a rubber substitute from alcohol during the 1930s. Standard Oil, which had patent agreements with Farben and received some help from that company, also developed a technology enabling it to begin production of synthetic rubber from petroleum, which was extremely cheap at that time. Three years prior to Pearl Harbor, Standard Oil urged the U.S. government (to no avail) to fund experimental plants to test the new technology. Rubber companies, particularly Goodyear and Goodrich, were also working on processes to make tires from synthetic rubber.

All of the early research on synthetic rubber came about because of the rubber cartel and the resulting high prices during the 1920s, and to some extent because of the IRRA cartel of the 1930s. In marked contrast to the fable we quoted at the beginning of this chapter, synthetic rubber was developed in response to the formation of cartels, *not* in response to potential hostilities with Japan.

THE EVE OF WAR, 1940–1941

Where did the United States stand in regard to synthetic rubber prior to its entry into World War II? In 1939, total world exports of plantation rubber amounted to 970,000 tons. Synthetic production was slightly more than 75,000 tons; the production of reclaimed rubber was approximately 100,000 tons. But the United States at that time had the capacity to produce 300,000 tons of reclaimed rubber.

While Germany led the world in the technology of producing synthetic rubber, the United States was not far behind. In 1940, technical experts in the United States were confident that within two years enough plants could be built to produce 600,000 tons of synthetic rubber, should the need for such a crash program come about. They felt this goal could be achieved at a cost of $100 to $200 million. All types of synthetic rubber cost three to five times more than natural rubber at the time—in part because of the state of the technology but also, to some extent, because of the small volume being produced.

The major synthetics being produced at the time were neoprene by DuPont and butadiene rubber such as Buna from Standard Oil and Ameripol from Goodrich. Because of neoprene's special features, such as resistance to oil and chemicals, DuPont was producing a considerable amount of it in its New Jersey plant. And, in 1940, DuPont was building another plant for the production of neoprene.

The major problem with neoprene, however, was that it was not really suitable for the production of tires, which accounted for 25 percent of all rubber consumption in the United States. While tires made from neoprene were wearing as well as those made from natural rubber in road tests and were superior in flexibility and age resistance, they would heat up much more rapidly and to much higher temperatures than other tires under loads. This was particularly a problem in the case of tires for trucks and for other military uses. It was thought that tires from butadiene would solve this problem. The Germans, who were making tires from Buna—a butadiene synthetic—claimed they did.

Butadiene could be made from grains, or almost any type of vegetable that could be converted into alcohol, or from petroleum, natural gas, coal, or butane. Germany, which had no petroleum, went the way of alcohol. In the United States, the most logical ingredient was petroleum, because it was so cheap. German chemists would have preferred to use petroleum but, because of a lack of supply, they couldn't.

In the United States, four companies—U.S. Rubber, Goodyear, Firestone, and Goodrich—were actively carrying out research on tires made with synthetic rubber. Standard Oil, which had exchanged oil patents with I.G. Farben of Germany for information and patent rights in the production of Buna, was doing research and building a plant in Baton Rouge, Louisiana, to manufacture Buna. The company offered the license to produce Buna to any rubber company that wished it. Firestone built a plant that was producing small quantities in 1940 and was, in late 1940, building a larger plant.

In June 1940, the president of Goodrich announced the production of tires made from the synthetic Ameripol, a name signifying a polymer made in America. Goodrich had begun its research into this process in 1929, eleven years before it would begin making tires. Experimental tests showed that Ameripol tires wore as well as tires made from natural rubber and, quite important, they were remarkably resistant to heat as well as to aging and sunlight.

At the same time that Goodrich announced its tires made from Ameripol, the president of Standard Oil announced the invention of a new synthetic rubber called Butyl. The company had been researching this process since 1936. In 1940, they were manufacturing small amounts of Butyl in a plant in New Jersey.

Thus, the synthetic rubber industry was in existence prior to World War II. If no emergency had occurred, the industry would have probably undergone a long period of slow development. New products and processes would have been developed and tested and refined and retested. Certainly costs would have fallen and technology improved. After a while, synthetic rubber would have been competitive with natural rubber and superior in many uses. A major industry would eventually have developed.

But of course an emergency did occur. The Japanese conquered the regions that produced 98 percent of all natural rubber and shut off all rubber supplies to the United States. The development of synthetic rubber followed a different pattern. But the point is that it was not developed in a government crash program. It evolved in the market in response to cartel-induced crises.

THE WAR YEARS

In 1941, the United States imported more than one million tons of natural rubber. With Japanese invasions in the Far East, imports fell to 271,000 tons in 1942, then to 34,000 tons in 1943. The production of synthetic was still quite low in 1941 and 1942. Reclaimed rubber, the facilities for which were developed during the rubber crisis of the 1920s, filled the gap while production capacity for synthetic rubber was built. Plant capacity for reclaimed rubber was 350,000 tons a year in 1942.

But by 1943 the production of synthetic rubber had risen to 234,000 tons, and in 1944 over a quarter of a million tons were produced. This rapid replacement of natural rubber, first by reclaimed then by synthetic rubber, indicates graphically that the technology was in place and available prior to Pearl Harbor. All that was needed was the construction of large-scale manufacturing facilities. By the end of 1942, most of the planned capacity was under construction.

We might ask what was the role of the U.S. government in the development of synthetic rubber? The fable is that the development of synthetic was the result of a massive government project. However, we have seen that this was not the case. The first act of the U.S. government concerning the rubber industry was to set up the Rubber Reserve Company (RRC) in 1940. The RRC then proceeded to spend $5 million trying unsuccessfully to develop a source of natural rubber in Brazil. In 1941, RRC planned to build, with the cooperation of private firms, synthetic rubber plants with a capacity to produce 100,000 tons a year. Although RRC abandoned the plan completely the same year, several of the involved companies went ahead with the plans.

Certainly when the war came, the primary financing of the manufacturing facilities came from the government. Such a rapid development of a massive new industry was an incredible feat—a feat that would have been unthinkable without a crisis such as the greatest war in history. It would appear then that the primary role of the government in the process was to provide the financing. The technology both for reclaimed and synthetic rubber was developed by private firms in response to artificially high rubber prices and in anticipation of future shortages due not to war but rather to cartels.

Basically the same story can be told for Germany, where the technology for making synthetic rubber was more advanced. Research into the feasibility of synthetic rubber had begun in 1927 in response to high prices rather than to government intervention. The research had begun long before the Nazis came to power. Certainly private research was encouraged and partially financed by the German government during the 1930s in anticipation of war. But the industry and the basic manufacturing capacity were developed privately, primarily by I.G. Farben.

The irony is that in Great Britain, where there had been no problem with high rubber prices—the British had caused the problem—there was no available domestic technology to produce either reclaimed or synthetic rubber. As *Fortune* noted in its August 1940 article on synthetic rubber: "England has consistently pooh-poohed the idea of synthetics, with a wary eye on its plantation empire in natural rubber." Of course, it "pooh-poohed" the idea. Since high rubber prices had not been a problem in England since 1910, British industry had no reason to try to adapt. Thus, the beginning of the war found England with a very small capacity for reclaimed rubber and a nonexistant synthetic rubber industry. Not until late 1943 were plants even licensed to produce synthetic rubber—and those would have a capacity of only 36,000 tons. No facilities were available in England until 1944. Practically all of England's rubber during the war had to be imported from the United States.

SUMMARY

So that's the story of the beginning of the synthetic rubber industry during World War II. The United States, which had experienced previous rubber crises in the form of cartel-induced shortages and extremely high prices for crude rubber, had the manufacturing facilities to produce reclaimed rubber when the war started. Moreover, U.S. firms also had the basic technology needed to produce synthetic rubber. The same was true in Germany. Certainly there was a great deal of haste and waste in exploiting synthetic rubber after the war began, but events prevented the orderly, efficient development of the industry.

It would seem that if the United States had not experienced previous rubber-price increases, the country would not have had available at the beginning of the war the technology to produce synthetic and reclaimed rubber when the supply of natural rubber was cut off. Certainly, Great Britain, which had not experienced previous rubber crises, did not have the technology; so England was dependent on the United States for its rubber requirements during the war.

It seems to us that this experience provides us with a very optimistic outlook for our future. With a functioning market, the producers responded to the cartels and reduced America's dependence on foreign suppliers with research into a substitute. We shall see that this pattern had been followed many times before.

THE TIMBER CRISIS

4

WE now go back to the turn of the century to examine another resource crisis in America. And it was a bona fide crisis. America was running out of its most important, most necessary, and (purportedly) most nonsubstitutable natural resource.

At the turn of the century, America was experiencing the greatest period of economic growth in its history—indeed, this was probably the greatest period of growth in the history of the world. But America was running out of one of the two primary ingredients for sustaining this growth—wood. (The other essential input was iron.) As reported by the doom merchants of the period, the reason was easy to see: we were cutting down forests much faster than they could be replaced.

According to the doom merchants, the railroads, the driving force behind the industrialization, were doomed. After all, the railroads accounted for 20–25 percent of annual timber consumption. Most of this wood was used to replace crossties; 15–20 percent of the crossties had to be replaced every year. You simply couldn't run a railroad without wood.

And, for most uses, there was apparently no substitute for wood. It appeared there were only two choices: (1) follow the lead of the U.S.

Much of this chapter is based on the work of Sherry H. Olson in *The Depletion Myth*. To the reader interested in more detailed information about America's timber crisis, we recommend this excellent book.

Forest Service, an important division of the Department of Agriculture, and force reforestation of the continent or (2) conserve wood by slowing down or ending the growth of the nation. Those were the only apparent choices. Only a fool couldn't see that these were the only solutions. Somebody had to do something and fast.

A few headlines from the *New York Times* during the first decade of the twentieth century give a picture of how we viewed the situation.

Dec. 31, 1900	"THE END OF LUMBER SUPPLY"
Jan. 6, 1905	"TIMBER FAMINE NEAR, SAYS ROOSEVELT [AND] NATIONAL FOREST SERVICE"
Aug. 31, 1908	"NEW PLAN TO SAVE NATIONAL FOREST. SENATOR SMOOT TO RECOMMEND THAT THEY BE TURNED OVER TO STATES, CITIES, AND COUNTIES. REFORESTRY THE OBJECT"
Oct. 31, 1908	"HICKORY DISAPPEARING, SUPPLY OF WOOD NEARS END—MUCH WASTED AND THERE'S NO SUBSTITUTE"
Dec. 7, 1908	"BANISH CHRISTMAS TREES, DR. MACARTHUR SAYS THIS HEATHENISH PRACTICE DENUDES FORESTS"
Dec. 16, 1908	"URGES LAWS TO SAVE TREES, FOREST WILL BE WIPED OUT IN TEN YEARS AT PRESENT RATE, WHIPPLE SAYS"

The headlines, reminiscent of those in the 1970s, convey the feeling at the time. And the feeling was utter gloom. Really, banning Christmas trees to save wood! Was nothing sacred? We can't recall such a draconian measure having been suggested even during the height of the oil crisis, although President Carter did refuse to light the White House Christmas tree in 1979. We all have to sacrifice during a crisis.

The U.S. Forest Service was still forecasting a resource disaster even as late as the early 1920s, when the crisis had been resolved. Sherry Olson, in *The Depletion Myth* (pp. 141–42), quotes a Forest Service publication of 1923:

> Directly or indirectly, every commodity of life will cost more because of the depleted supply of forest products. Every Ameri-

can will pay an unnecessarily large part of his income for shelter, and food, and clothing and fuel, transportation and amusements, necessities and luxuries alike, because wood will be no longer plentiful and near at hand.

This economic punishment will increase in severity as time goes on. There is only one way by which its pressure can be relieved and removed, and that is by growing enough timber for the national needs.

Change "wood" to "oil" and the last sentence to ". . . that is by becoming self-sufficient in oil." A report of the Department of Energy in 1979? A speech by the energy czar in 1975? Remember? We really did have an energy czar in 1975.

But there was clearly a problem in 1900. Public officials, the media, the president, and the informed public were justifiably worried about it. If people continued to consume timber at the same rate and if the growth rate of timber did not increase significantly, our forests would be quickly depleted. We would be a second rate economic power. We would become practically a "banana republic" except we couldn't grow bananas very well in our climate.

Well, where do we stand today? When was the last time you worried about running out of wood? Out of lumber? Possibly you experienced a timber crisis when you were caught short while building a dog house on Saturday afternoon and the lumber yards were closed. Certainly lumber prices rise and fall in response to building booms and busts. But Americans now worry about other kinds of conservation issues—energy, water, pollution, soil exhaustion—rather than timber.

Why aren't people lining up at the Smithsonian to look at America's last living tree? What happened to the timber crisis? What caused it? More significantly, what ended it? How did such a serious national problem with such dire consequences become practically inconsequential? Let's face it. It was a serious problem; but it did end—and in a relatively short period of time. Let's see what happened.

EVOLUTION OF A CRISIS, 1865–1896

After the Civil War, America began the greatest economic expansion in history. In less than thirty years, the railroads spanned a continent. Prairie crossroads became towns, towns became cities, and cities became metropolises. The so-called robber barons were investing and building industrial empires at an unprecedented rate.

The economic expansion required labor; and labor came, by the millions in the form of the "poor and huddled masses" from Europe and Asia. Rapid growth also required iron, steel, coal, and oil—all in increasing amounts. Pittsburgh made iron and steel from the seemingly unlimited ore deposits of Minnesota. Men discovered coal seams in the northern Appalachian Mountains that would last 500 years at prevailing rates of depletion. When the Pennsylvania oil fields petered out, seemingly infinite deposits were found in Texas. A single well, Spindletop, outside of Beaumont, Texas, pumped more oil in its first year of operation than had been previously pumped from the earth. Everything was apparently unlimited. That is, almost everything.

If the nation was built with iron, it was also built with wood. If the nation moved on iron rails, it also moved on wood ties. And Pittsburgh couldn't forge timber. Neither could Cleveland, Chicago, or New York.

Timber had to be grown; and that took time, a long time. Much more time than late nineteenth-century use would allow. We were using up our forests faster than they could grow. Why?

One problem, of course, was the depletion of eastern forests to make room for farms prior to the Civil War. For a long time, the prevailing method of extracting timber was clear cutting. This technique also led to forest fires, further depleting the forests. Furthermore, such cutting was not conducive to reforestation. Indeed, the railroads had switched from wood to coal for fuel by the end of the Civil War, partially as a result of this problem.

Wood, however, was a major ingredient in the expansion following that war. It had many advantages as a building material. In most areas, it was a low cost material; since wood was light relative to its size, it was inexpensive to ship. Unskilled labor, using relatively simple equipment at the building site, could handle the material quite easily. Most significantly, however, it was abundant.

During the years following the Civil War, American woodworking machinery became the most advanced in the world. American power saws were the fastest anywhere. American mills could handle more timber in less time, by far, than any other mills anywhere in the world.

But it is important to note that no other country adopted the American technology. Although they were extremely fast, American saws turned a very large proportion of the lumber into sawdust. European saws were much slower and required far more labor but returned considerably less sawdust. Nathan Rosenberg, an expert on technological change in America, quotes an observer familiar with American and British woodworking in the 1870s as remarking that "lumber manufacture, from the log to the finished state, is, in America, characterized by a waste that can truly be called criminal." The oil guzzlers of the 1970s were the wood guzzlers of the 1870s.

But were the methods used by Americans in the 1870s really "criminal" or even wasteful? Certainly, the methods used in America would indeed have been wasteful in England or France at that time. In Western Europe at the end of the nineteenth century, timber was very scarce and very expensive. On the other hand, labor was relatively cheap. Europeans conserved wood and expended labor.

In America, timber was abundant and therefore cheap. Conversely, because of the relatively small population and the opportunities available in the frontier, labor was very expensive. So American business expended wood and conserved labor as it built a nation. Whenever possible, Americans substituted the abundant wood for the scarce labor. And they continued to do so, until wood became expensive.

Businesses weren't the only guilty parties. Consumers "wasted" wood also. Fireplaces were designed for very large logs, which saved labor time in cutting but burned up a lot of wood relative to the heat provided. More efficient stoves, like those used in Europe, were more expensive and required more labor to prepare the logs. So, as you would expect, the use of these stoves was not widespread in the United States until wood prices rose considerably.

Builders in America used wood for purposes not dreamed of in Europe, where metal or stone would have been used. Houses were constructed using labor-saving, wood-guzzling technology. As the frontier moved west, town after town sprung up. And they were built entirely of wood. The buildings weren't built to last, but they went up fast, and it didn't take much labor to get them built.

But don't call these methods inefficient. They were very efficient. Businesses and consumers were smart. They were niggardly with the expensive factors of production—labor and time. To conserve these expensive resources, they were profligate with the abundant, cheap, and easily used natural resource—timber. And as industrial growth increased, the rate of depletion of wood increased also.

But the real wood users, the major depleters during this period, were the railroads. From the 1870s to 1900, the railroads consumed as much as one-fourth of the annual timber production in the United States. The railroads being built across the prairies were much more wood intensive than the older eastern railroads. Everything except the rails, spikes, car wheels, and locomotives was made of wood.

The reason was simple. These railroads were built through areas that were rather sparsely populated. To survive, they had to begin to yield a return on the investment quickly. So what would the owners do? Clearly, they were induced to build rapidly, lightly, and cheaply. There would be time enough to rebuild substantially when population and traffic increased. Also, both labor and capital were more scarce on the prairie and hence more expensive than in the East. These expensive resources had to be carefully conserved.

Wood was the answer. It was light, easily worked, and, until the 1890s, cheap. Moreover, it could be replaced and repaired more easily. So the prairie railroads began to use wood in great volume. In addition to using wood for crossties, the railroads used wood for bridges, tunnels, fences, culverts, and telegraph poles. Round timbers were frequently used in bridge construction to save sawing, a technique that used a lot of wood but saved time and labor.

The pattern was established. The nation was experiencing the most rapid growth in its history. And the railroads, one of the most wood-intensive sectors of the economy, were the major industry.

In all areas, but especially in the westward expansion, labor was relatively expensive. So was capital. These had to be conserved. The answer was to build with wood, and they did.

But by 1880, only a fool would have suggested that timber could continue to be used at this rate for very long without a gigantic increase in timber production. If this prevailing trend continued, the nation would run out of wood. No wood, no growth, no more prosperity.

The problem was that no good substitute was available. And because it rotted, wood was almost impossible to recycle. In short, a timber famine was inevitable, and economic collapse (or stagnation) would surely follow. Or so the doom merchants of the time told us.

THE RAILROAD EXPERIMENT, 1880–1896

Since the railroads were the largest consumers of wood in the country, they were among the first to begin preparations for the time when timber prices would start climbing. Three types of response were thought to be possible: (1) substituting alternative materials for the wood currently used, either different types of wood or steel and concrete; (2) improving design to conserve wood; or (3) using chemical preservation to extend the life of wood.

There were several areas of wood use where one or more of these possibilities might be applied. Since crossties were the major source of wood consumption, this was a possible area for study. The railroads also used an extremely large amount of timber for bridges, piling, car construction, telegraph poles, fences, tunnels, wharves, buildings, and platforms. The most promising area for study by the railroads, when they became convinced that wood would become increasingly scarce, was increasing the efficiency of wood use.

Prior to 1896, the railroads made great progress in acquiring knowledge about the properties of wood and wood substitutes. This knowledge made it possible to substitute less scarce grades of wood and in some instances steel and concrete for the scarcer woods in some uses. Research on track stress allowed some conservation of crossties. It was found that a significant economy in wood use could be achieved in two ways: (1) proper species selection for the appropriate use and (2) correct wood seasoning to develop wood strength. For example, proper air seasoning was shown to reduce wood decay and lengthen the useful life of the wood. So by 1896, the railroads could economize on wood use through seasoning, species selection, and alternative design. But except in some regions in which timber was extremely scarce, there was little incentive to actually implement wood conservation techniques—and considerable incentive not to—until the price of wood rose much higher.

Bridge design was an important area that could yield great savings in wood consumption. The railroad bridges constructed after the Civil War used designs developed for construction during that war. As you can imagine, these designs were developed for rapid construction with little attention paid to wood conservation. Such methods were ideal for the prairie railroads. They sacrificed materials to gain speed in construction and save labor. To test a new bridge design, the designer would just build the bridge, load a car with iron, and pull it back and forth over the bridge, increasing its load until the bridge collapsed. The breaking weight per linear foot was recorded. Consequently, since the weakest part of the bridge collapsed, bridges were over-designed or overstressed, with a resulting over-usage of wood. When wood was cheap, a lot of it was used.

Advances in metallurgy showed that steel or iron bridges were, in many places, more cost effective than those made of wood. As many hastily built wooden bridges reached the end of their lives and as the price of wood rose, more and more were being replaced by metal bridges. The first general substitution of metal bridges for wood took place in the 1890s in regions where wood had always been expensive—particularly the Middle West. This replacement began even before the general increase in the price of timber. But while the price of timber was not rising, the price of iron was falling during this period. So the price of wood relative to iron rose, and some substitution was economical.

One use where substitution occurred was the construction of culverts. Between 1888 and 1895, 500 wood culverts a year were replaced. Four-fifths of the replacements were built with iron; the remainder were made from used bridge timber.

Prior to 1900, the railroads made a great deal of progress in developing designs that used less timber in wooden trestles. The type of testing we described, in which individual segments were not designed and tested independently, led to much more wood being used in a trestle than was necessary. So as knowledge of bridge construction advanced, the railroads were able to save considerably on the amount of timber used.

Another innovation that allowed the railroads to save on timber use was wood preservation. As you would expect, the technology of preserving wood from rot was much more advanced in Europe, where wood was extremely scarce, than in America, where it was much more abundant. The first American railroads that experimented to any great extent with preservation of crossties were located in the old settlement areas around Boston, New York, and Philadelphia and on the prairies. In both areas, timber, as you might expect, was more expensive than in other areas of the country. Prior to 1880, several different methods of preservation were tried, with little success. But in 1881, three prairie railroads, the Sante Fe, Union Pacific, and Rock Island (all located in areas characterized by high timber prices), developed a process for preserving crossties. However, at that time the high cost of preservation relative to the cost of timber made tie preservation uneconomical in most areas.

To illustrate why it was not economical to preserve timber, let us provide a typical example from that period. In 1883, the Burlington railroad considered treating hemlock ties with zinc oxide so they could be used in place of the more expensive oak ties. Hemlock ties cost 24 cents each. The treatment added another 24 cents and additional costs were between 6 and 12 cents, depending on the location. The total cost of a treated hemlock tie was between 54 and 60 cents, a figure that did not differ substantially from the cost of an oak tie. Since the expected life was the same—about eight years—for either type of tie, preservation was not adopted.

An important advance in 1885 came in a report of a special committee of the American Society of Civil Engineers. This report concluded that many sources of timber supply were being rapidly depleted. It predicted generally increasing timber prices and growing difficulty in obtaining wood. The report made available the more advanced European processes for wood preservation, especially creosoting.

So although conditions were changing, in all but a few regions where timber was especially expensive it was not economical to practice preservation. Sherry Olson (p. 67), quoting a report of the American Society of Civil Engineers, notes:

> So long as wood was cheap, the cost of efficient preparation, including interest on plant and price of antiseptics, was so great in proportion to the ruling timber prices . . . timber preparation did not pay. It was cheaper to let it rot in the good old way.

Preservation would not be economical until timber prices rose. Predictions about future wood prices forced the railroads to think about preservation and other types of wood conservation. But in most areas of the United States, economic conditions simply did not justify its practice. Not yet at least.

In 1896, conditions changed—wood prices began to rise rapidly. The earlier research undertaken by the railroads would begin to pay dividends.

THE RAILROADS ADAPT, 1896–1914

In 1896, timber prices began to rise. As the price of wood rose between 1896 and 1907 (the price of crosstie stumpage increased 500–800 percent during this period), the relative price of substitutes, such as concrete and steel, fell. The railroads now began to adapt; slowly at first, rapidly later on. If the possibility of timber famine induced research in conservation methods, rising prices caused the new developments to be used.

At first the railroads, at the urging of the U.S. Forest Service, considered reforestation of the country as a remedy. Some railroads even went so far as to invest in forests. But they soon realized that this was not the answer. The production of wood took longer than they and the Forest Service had at first believed, and the projects proved uneconomical, even with the higher prices of timber. Almost all the railroads abandoned their forestation projects.

The railroads become increasingly disillusioned with the recommendations of the Forest Service. During this period, they found that the real remedy lay in more efficient and more limited use of timber. Reduced consumption replaced increased production as the solution. Substitution was the answer. Olson (p. 97) quotes an executive of the Pennsylvania Railroad, who explained in 1910:

> So far, much less emphasis has been placed on the equally important question of reducing the consumption of forest products. It is very well to make an area produce two sticks of timber where before there was but one; still, it is just as good lumber economy to double the life of the first stick, and there is the added advantage of an immense saving to the consumer.

So more and more the railroads turned to wood preservation and more efficient uses of timber. Many of the innovations were truly ingenious. Many new, more plentiful species of timber were found to be suitable for crossties after preservation was done. Research showed that ties made of hardwood, such as untreated white oak, could be saved for steep grades, sharp turns, and heavy traffic areas where the ties wore out before they rotted. Treated softer woods could be used in less demanding places. New, more efficient methods of sawing ties were found. These methods reduced the amount of wood used in a given tie. Furthermore, sawing instead of hewing the ties allowed wood that was previously scrap or chips to be used for boards and flooring. All sizes of trees could then be used for ties, whereas hewing of ties required the trees to be eleven to fifteen inches in diameter.

During this transition period, seasoning and preservation of much of the wood destined both for ties and for other uses became quite widespread. Again, these processes permitted considerable saving in timber. But in addition to rotting out, crossties wore out because of mechanical stress. From 1900 to 1914, many innovations were introduced to reduce the stress on ties. For example, tie plates and new types of fastening were designed to protect ties from wear. Different types of fastening and plates were added to protect the wood fibers. More scientific track design also was used to conserve wood.

From 1900 to 1914, the railroads paid a great deal of attention to substitution of other materials for wood. Iron, steel, and concrete were substituted in many uses. For example, there was a rapid shift from all-wood to all-metal cars between 1900 and 1914. As we noted earlier, there was a substitution away from wood in bridge construction. When wood was used in bridge repair and construction, it was treated wood.

We could go on and enumerate the different methods the railroads used to adapt to higher wood prices, but there would be little point in doing so. The major point is, as Sherry Olson notes (p. 7), that the response of the railroads to the timber crisis "demonstrates that the industrial consumer has substantial power to bring about greater efficiency in the use of resources and to confound predictions that look only at his past habits and fail to take into account his powers of choice and change." In other words, consumers are not at the mercy of suppliers.

THE ROLE OF THE U.S. FOREST SERVICE, 1898–1920

What was the role of the government during the crisis? Let's look at what the Forest Service was doing at the time. Until 1898, the U.S. Forest Service, established to protect and increase the nation's forests, was little more than a research organization. It carried out research both in wood conservation and in efficient forestry methods. But the budget was very small and little was accomplished.

In 1898, Gifford Pinchot, later to be known as the great conserva-
tionist, became chief of the Forest Service. Two statements from the
service after Pinchot became chief illustrate its position: "We have
never been so near to the exhaustion of our lumber supply," and "the
forest of the private owners will have to be set in order if the over-
whelming calamity of a timber famine is to be kept from the nation"
(Olson, p. 72). With a couple of word changes, the two statements
could have come from the Department of Energy in 1979, couldn't
they? Let's look at what the Forest Service wanted to do.

To understand what the service recommended, we must first understand the basic theory their plans were based on. The main point
was that depletion of the forests was causing wood prices to rise.
Starting in 1896, timber prices, especially the prices of replacement
railroad ties, began to increase. These rising prices pointed to a de-
creasing supply of timber.

Since the Forest Service and many people interested in the problem assumed that the quantity of wood (per capita) demanded by the
economy was fixed, regardless of price, the price of wood depended
upon conditions of supply. Now, admittedly, a decrease in the supply
of something will increase its price. But the Forest Service had a
different interpretation. And it was a simple theory. Wrong, but
simple.

According to the Forest Service, as timber was exhausted in one
area, customers had to buy timber from another, more remote area,
and therefore had to pay a higher price. The price remained at the new
level until that region was depleted and a new timber region brought
in, at an even higher price. People used the same amount of wood,
regardless of price. If the Forest Service didn't do something, the
nation would be denuded, except for the trees in museums.

Based on this line of reasoning, the only salvation was to fill the
gap between the amount of wood demanded and the amount supplied.
Clearly, the only solution for the Forest Service—an agency staffed
primarily by foresters—was increased planting and growing. Silviculture would reforest the nation and save it from its own greed and
waste. And a massive reforestation it would have to be, since the
nation was using annually 40 cubic feet of timber per capita, while the
growth of the forests produced only 13 cubic feet per capita annually.

So you can see that the gapsmanship approach is not just a phe-
nomenon of the past decade. It has a long, though not particularly

distinguished, history. If a resource is being used up only two things can be done: find (or grow) more of the stuff or force people to use less. Either way, the gap must be closed.

Although some of the Forest Service's resources were used for product research, most of its efforts went into forestry and, after 1905, to administering the national forests. By 1912, only 4–5 percent of the total budget was devoted to forest products, down from 12 percent in 1904. The primary interest of the Forest Service was how to grow more trees.

For a time, the Forest Service even interested the railroads in forestry as a solution to the problem. Many of the railroads promoted and even practiced forestry. After all, the experts were saying that more efficient forestry was the solution, and the railroads believed the experts. Wouldn't you have believed? But the experts were wrong, as the railroads soon discovered.

During the crucial period between 1900 and 1915, the Forest Service gave the railroads some more poor advice, in addition to encouraging them to promote and practice forestry. For example, foresters encouraged the railroads to use half round ties and short, eight-foot ties, in order to conserve wood. The railroads learned that such ties actually used more wood. The heavier, longer rectangular ties were more economical and gave longer service. Also, the Forest Service urged tie makers to use trees with larger diameters than was customary, in order to save the smaller trees for other, higher valued use. That, of course, meant that the service was recommending smaller ties made from larger trees, an economic contradiction that the railroads didn't buy.

The Forest Service also recommended planting faster-growing species of trees. This recommendation was followed, but it was an economic failure. All in all, the advice given by the service was not very effective. According to Olson (pp. 96–97):

> The silviculturists continued through World War I to predict rising prices for wood, critical shortages, and a painful "wood famine." They continued to agitate for large investments in plantations and forest holdings as profitable and patriotic ventures . . . [The railroads] were advised to adopt practices in line with an idealized concept of "good forestry," instead of forest practices that would actually promote railroad economies.

The Crisis Is Over

So that's our story. By 1922, the problem was virtually solved. With the exception of a brief problem in housing, the shortages disappeared. Wood prices rose sharply between 1915 and 1920, then continued to rise gradually relative to the prices of alternative materials. But there was no alarm. Not many predicted a timber famine or forest exhaustion.

The Forest Service continued to emphasize silviculture and management of the national forests. The railroads, which were the biggest timber users, became the greatest economizers. Railroad consumption fell from 20–25 percent of the timber cut in 1909 to 3 or 4 percent (excluding pulpwood) in the 1960s.

Other users followed the lead of the railroads in wood conservation. High timber prices encouraged a shift from wood to other building materials in the construction industries. Wood preservation, begun by the railroads, extended the life of wood in other uses, such as fence posts, telephone poles, and buildings.

To appreciate the shift in emphasis, consider the fact that in 1911 the Forest Service investigated the "hickory problem." The annual hickory cut was depleting 3 percent of the U.S. supply (which was the world supply) each year. There was no satisfactory substitute, and hickory trees would soon disappear. Many uses of hickory should be discouraged.

Forty years later the Forest Service formed the Hickory Group to again attack the hickory problem. However, this time the problem was different. Because of the low demand for hickory, hickory trees were taking over the eastern hardwood forests—up to 30 percent of the timber. The Hickory Group was formed to encourage consumer demand for hickory. So much for depletion.

Was there a crisis? Certainly. Unquestionably, timber use could not have continued at the same rate without total depletion, and fairly quickly. There was a problem, and something did have to be done. However, the U.S. Forest Service was of little use. The primary consumers of wood, led by the railroads, adapted their levels of consumption through technological change.

They substituted other materials for wood when the relative price of timber rose. Under the same incentive, they were able to extend the effective life of the wood they did use and to use wood more efficiently.

So market forces overcame this crisis. No one had to force consumers to economize and substitute. Instead it was a case of the users of wood wanting to make a profit and responding to scarcity and price change. The famine was over. As a matter of fact, it never really came.

AMERICA'S FIRST OIL CRISIS

5

DURING the past decade, we have heard much about alternative energy sources and synfuels. However, few people remember that petroleum is itself an "alternative energy source." Petroleum—or, as it was called, "rock oil"—was the alternative energy source of the nineteenth century.

Prior to the Civil War, America lubricated its machinery and fueled its lamps with oil from whales. Sperm oil, obtained from the sperm whale, was the best illuminant available at the time. But oil from other types of whales, because it was considerably cheaper than sperm oil, was widely used also. At the time, these oils were practically "essential" to an industrializing economy.

Nonetheless, during and after the Civil War, the whaling industry experienced a rapid decline. Table 3 shows some illustrative figures for oil production and the size of the American whaling fleet that should demonstrate the decline in this previously important industry.

What led to such a dramatic decline? Why did such an important industry become so insignificant? Many writers have argued that the discovery of petroleum led to the demise of the whaling industry. For example, in *The Whalers* (p. 150), A.B.C. Whipple asserted that:

> It is a safe assumption that in 1859 very few, if any, whalemen had heard the name Edwin L. Drake. And there was no reason why they should have, for Drake was an obscure entrepreneur. But

· over the next decades every whaleman would come to know, and curse, Drake's name. For on August 27 of 1859, his Seneca Oil Company succeeded in extracting petroleum from the earth by drilling 69 feet down into the soil near Titusville, Pennsylvania. In so doing he put an end to Yankee whaling industry just as surely as if he had drilled a hole in the hold of every whaleship.

The same theme was expressed by F. D. Ommanney (p. 92) in *Lost Leviathan*.

But in 1859 the greatest and most lasting blow was struck at the whaling fleet. This was the discovery of petroleum and the production of oil from mineral sources which competed with sperm oil and, in the end, drove it off the market as a fuel and illuminant.

Unquestionably, petroleum did replace the previously necessary sperm and whale oil as the primary illuminant and lubricant during the decade after the Civil War. But many who have written about the rise of the petroleum industry tell a different story from that told by the chroniclers of the demise of whaling. For example, in the centennial issue of *World Oil* (p. 135), we find the following:

Oil had been known since the beginning of history. The pitch used to caulk Noah's Ark undoubtedly was petroleum. Many other simple uses are recorded in the early pages of history and down through the centuries. Early American settlers found Indians skimming oil from seeps and using it for both internal and external medicine. A few enterprising American business pioneers were selling "Rock Oil" as medicine by the middle of the 19th Century. Their sources of supply were seepages or salt brine wells in which they were "unfortunate" enough to find oil.

However, no one gave any serious study to the commercial possibilities of oil until the simultaneous beginnings of the Age of Light and the Machine Age *created the world's first and most serious oil shortage.* [Emphasis added.]

Keep in mind that the preceding quotation was published in 1959, fourteen years before our own serious oil shortage. However, the important assertion made in this article was that the rise of the petroleum industry was itself the result of a shortage of whale oil—America's first oil crisis.

TABLE 3   THE AMERICAN WHALING INDUSTRY, 1856–1876

| | Whale Industry Production | |
Year	Sperm Oil Production (barrels)	Whale Oil Production (barrels)
1856	80,941	197,890
1861	68,932	133,717
1866	36,663	74,302
1876	39,811	33,010

| | The Whaling Fleet | |
Year	Number of Whaling Vessels	Tonnage
1856	635	199,141
1861	514	158,745
1866	263	68,536
1876	169	38,883

SOURCE: Walter S. Tower, *A History of the American Whale Fishery*, pp. 121, 126.

Which was it? Did the rise of the petroleum industry sink the whaling industry? Or, was the advent of the oil industry the result of a shortage in whale oil? Was there a whale oil crisis? Let's look at some historical evidence.

THE EARLY WHALING INDUSTRY

The first whaling in North America was done by Indians on the East and West coasts, long before Europeans arrived. The search for whales probably began with the killing of stranded whales, for which the Indians kept watch. After killing the whale, they used the oil for heat and illumination, the meat for food, and the bones for building.

After Europeans settled New England, they also kept watch for and killed stranded whales. Not long after the settlement of New England, American whalers began to go to sea and hunt whales, probably because relative to the expanding population, fewer and fewer whales were becoming stranded in coastal bays.

New Englanders became familiar with the new (to them) and superior sperm whale when one of their species became stranded close to shore. All parties involved—Indians, settlers, and the Crown—claimed the whale. The next sperm whale captured was struck and killed in 1712 by a boat hunting other types of whales in the Atlantic. As people became familiar with the superiority of sperm oil as an illuminant and as certain other types of whale were becoming scarce, whalers increasingly searched for sperm whales. A new industry was born.

As boats ventured farther and farther out into the ocean, they consequently were built larger and larger. The whaleboats progressed from rowboats with a single sail to ships up to 50 tons and 40 feet long with multiple sails. Early in the eighteenth century, whale ships could be fitted for voyages up to seven weeks long.

The demand for whale products in England and the colonies increased rapidly during the first half of the eighteenth century. Consequently, the price of sperm oil rose substantially during the century until the beginning of the Revolutionary War. In 1731, the price of sperm oil was 7 pounds sterling per ton. In 1768, the price had risen to 17 pounds sterling per ton; at the beginning of the war, the price was over 40 pounds sterling. Since the index of consumer prices remained relatively stable in this period, the increase was large in both nominal and real terms.

As we would expect, the increase in price led to a substantial increase in the number of whaling vessels. By the start of the war, 60 ships were sailing from New Bedford alone, making that city the capital of the North American whaling industry, with Nantucket a close second.

Since whaling ships could not leave port during the Revolutionary War because of the high probability of being sunk by British ships, the New England whaling industry lay dormant from 1776 to 1784. But when the whaling fleet was rebuilt, the whalers found that the whale population had increased during the period of no hunting. By

1788, the New England fleet reached the same size as before the war. And by this time, whalers were venturing around Cape Horn into the Pacific Ocean.

The increased hunting had the obvious consequence. Whales were becoming increasingly scarce in the Atlantic. Further contributing to the problems of the whaling industry, Great Britain, in an effort to build its own whaling industry, imposed a tariff of eighteen pounds sterling per barrel on imported oil. (The U.S. auto industry didn't invent this tactic. It has been around for centuries.) So this tariff effectively eliminated British markets. France, however, had in the meantime become a good market, and the demand in the United States was increasing. As we would expect, ships became larger and larger, and whalers were now able to undertake voyages of up to three years.

At the beginning of the nineteenth century, the U.S. whale oil industry was hit with three blows. First, the French Revolution closed the French market. Then, in 1807, because of privateers, the Embargo Act prohibited whalers from leaving port. Finally, during the war of 1812, the British fleet practically destroyed the American whaling fleet.

But after the war of 1812, the whaling fleet began once more to increase rapidly. The number of ships (though not tonnage) peaked in 1846 when 729 American whaling ships were afloat. At the time, the price of sperm oil was 88 cents a barrel, and the price of whale oil was 33 cents a barrel, still relatively cheap. But cheap oil couldn't continue. High volume whaling was rapidly depleting the raw material—the whales. The more whales killed, the fewer there were to reproduce. The birthrate declined dramatically, as you would expect. Spurred on by the declining whale population, the whaling ships sailed farther and farther from New England. Whaling became more and more efficient. But no matter how efficient the whalers were, the whales wouldn't cooperate by reproducing at a more rapid rate. Regardless of the efficiency of the whaling fleet, the whales just weren't there in the numbers they had been in the past.

By the 1840s, American whalers covered the sea. The Pacific was heavily hunted. During the 1830s and 1840s, there were at times more than a hundred ships off the coast of Japan alone. And, of course, the heavy hunting clearly decreased the supply of whales even further. Once again, America was using up an important natural resource. And as in the case for all natural resources, when the supply of whales decreased, the price of whale oil began to increase.

How High Can Oil Prices Go?

By 1850, the price of sperm oil had risen to $1.20 a barrel, and that of whale oil to 49 cents, increases of 36 and 48 percent, respectively, over a four-year period. (The increases in real terms were essentially the same since the price index remained practically unchanged over this period.) By 1856, the price of sperm oil had risen to $1.62, an increase of 84 percent over the ten-year period; the price of whale oil went to 80 cents, an increase of 143 percent over the same period. While the prices of sperm and other whale oil fell somewhat from 1856 until the beginning of the Civil War, the price in real terms fell only about 5 percent, since the price index declined over this period. In any case, in 1860 the price of oil was substantially above what it had been 20 years before.

As you would expect, induced by the rising price of oil, even more ships went to sea to hunt the whales. Total ship tonnage employed in whaling increased from 171,484 tons (543 ships) in 1850 to a peak of 208,299 tons in 1854. Tonnage remained above 200,000 tons as late as 1858, the year before the discovery of petroleum.

But increased hunting did not mean increased oil production for the whaling fleet. Although the price of oil remained relatively high and the whaling fleet remained large, whales grew increasingly scarce and more difficult to find. Just before the Civil War, there seemed to be no solution in sight. How could a country fight a war without lubricants? Whale and sperm oil was "essential" and we were about to run out of it.

The Beginning of the Age of Petroleum

Of course, there was a solution in sight. As a matter of fact, the solution was just around the corner. As we know now, the solution was crude petroleum. And we know also that petroleum quickly became not only superior to whale oil as a lubricant and illuminant but also cheaper.

As noted earlier, petroleum had been known since the dawn of time. People knew it could be used for caulking, and its medicinal properties were widely known early in the nineteenth century. And as we will show, by the late 1850s people knew how to use petroleum as an illuminant and lubricant. The problem was, people didn't know how to get it out of the ground in any significant quantities.

In the early part of the 1800s, no one really experimented with petroleum as an illuminant or lubricant, because whale and sperm oil was so cheap. There was no need for a substitute oil when cheap whale oil was readily available. But when the machine age began, the demand for lighting increased and whales became scarcer. Consequently, the price of whale oil rose, and people began to search for a suitable substitute. Crude petroleum was seen by some persons to have possibilities as a solution to the whale oil crisis as early as 1853.

By 1859, A.C. Ferris was actively working with petroleum as an illuminant in New York. He was able to make fuel from oil and he greatly improved the kerosene lamp. But he had trouble finding a supply. He was importing oil from as far away as Canada, California, and even the East Indies. This oil, as did all other oil, came from seepages and from wells that were dug rather than drilled. Ferris himself tried unsuccessfully to dig for oil in the brine area of western Pennsylvania. But don't feel too sorry for him; he later became one of the pioneers in the new petroleum industry.

Even earlier, in 1853, George H. Bissell, a journalist and teacher, had become interested in what was then called "rock oil" when he became convinced that this oil would make an excellent illuminant. So convinced was he, that he purchased land on Oil Creek in Pennsylvania, an area known for its frequent oil seepage. Bissell and some other men joined together in the Pennsylvania Oil Company and were soon selling oil from seepages on their property at $1.50 a gallon. In 1855, the company hired a famous scientist, Benjamin Silliman, to analyze the properties of oil. Silliman reported that oil would make an excellent illuminant and would also be a good lubricant.

Bissell and some of his partners planned to drill for oil in 1857 using methods that others used to drill for water and salt brine. But since some of the stockholders in the Pennsylvania Oil Company objected strenuously to the venture, Bissell had to reorganize the company as the Seneca Oil Company. The company was continually plagued by disturbances over financing. It then hired Edwin L. Drake, a retired railroad conductor who was totally unfamiliar with the technology of drilling wells, to drill a well on Bissell's property near Titusville, Pennsylvania. Fortunately, Drake hired William Smith, an experienced well driller, to carry out the actual drilling. The crew consisted of Smith's two young sons. On August 27, 1859, late on a Sunday afternoon, this group struck oil, made history, and changed the world.

Even before Bissell and Silliman began exploring the properties of oil, Samuel Kier of Tarentum, Pennsylvania, then the center of a large salt well region, became interested in petroleum. In 1844, the salt brine wells in the area began to produce a nuisance in the form of sludge, which had to be drained off onto the ground or into a canal. When the sludge caught fire one day, people recognized that this oil would burn. By 1846, many people were burning the oil in their lamps even though it was smokey and smelled bad. It did, however, give off a good light and the price was right—the stuff was free for the taking.

Kier, who was selling petroleum, or rock oil, as a medicine, sent a sample to a chemist in Philadelphia, who reported that the oil would make a good illuminant and designed a still that might prove suitable for refining. Acting on these plans, Kier in 1854 built the first oil refinery in America in Pittsburgh, Pennsylvania. The refined oil was sold as a lighting oil. But the oil still stank when it was burned even though it did illuminate well. It also stank when being refined—so badly that the neighbors forced Pittsburgh's city officials to run both Kier and his refinery out of the city. Kier rebuilt the refinery out of the city and sold a considerable amount of lamp oil. He actually refined much of the oil from Drake's first well after 1859. Although he never could eliminate the bad odor, he did improve it. It was left to Silliman to develop the refining process further.

By 1859, there were 53 other refineries operating in the United States, but these refineries were designed to produce coal oil. The refining process, developed by Dr. James Young in Scotland, produced illuminants and lubricants from shale, peat, and coal. While some of these coal oil refineries went out of business after the Pennsylvania oil field came in, many were transformed into petroleum refineries.

After Drake's well came in, many others began drilling in the area. Thousands of people were attracted to the region almost immediately. Very quickly, well after well came in. Less than one year after Drake's well hit, oil was selling for $10 a barrel. At the end of 1861, it was selling for 10 cents a barrel. By late 1860, there were 15 refineries in the area; three years later there were 61. The world's first oil glut occurred. The price was so low that people all over the country were introduced to oil as a cheap, efficient, and reliable illuminant and lubricant.

The demands of a rapidly expanding manufacturing industry increased the demand for oil. Production leaped from a rate of 1,200 barrels a day in 1860 to more than 5,000 a day in 1861. On November 14, 1861, landowners in the Pennsylvania oil field met to organize and take measures to raise the price of oil. All business was to pass through a central authority. At the next meeting, the Oil Creek Association was formed to regulate production; and in January, 1862, the organization set the price of oil at $4 a barrel, up $3.90 from 1861. The first OPEC had emerged. At first, they sold little oil. But by the end of 1862, because of the increased demand, the market price actually became $4 a barrel. The price steadily increased thereafter. It remained high, though, not because of the loosely formed cartel, which soon broke up, but because demand kept increasing as people became more familiar with the properties of oil. By the end of the Civil War, petroleum was the sixth most important export of the United States, ranking behind only gold, corn, tobacco, wheat, and flour. Certainly oil had become an important commodity, and it was destined to become more and more important over time.

What was happening in the whaling industry as the petroleum industry was expanding? During the Civil War, the American whaling fleet was virtually destroyed. Confederate warships, the *Shenandoah* and the *Alabama*, sank a huge number of whalers both in the Atlantic and the Pacific. The remainder stayed in port to avoid being sunk. Many of the older whaling ships were loaded with stones and sunk by the U.S. Navy in Charleston harbor as part of the blockade of Southern ports during the war.

There was a brief revival in whaling after the war when the price of whale oil went to $2.50 a gallon. The number of whaling ships recovered to 253, but the number of whales was simply too small; whales were just too hard to find. Whaling as a major industry was dead by the 1870s. It died, just as the production of "whale-sized" automobiles died as a major industry a hundred years later, because of a resource crisis. But if whaling had peaked in tonnage and number of ships years before the first oil well came in, could the decline of whaling as a major industry be blamed on the discovery of petroleum?

RECONCILIATION

Returning to the question we posed at the beginning of the chapter, what can we conclude about the beginning of the age of petroleum? Did the discovery of petroleum destroy whaling or did petroleum arise as a result of an oil (whale oil) crisis? Certainly, we can agree that the increased scarcity of whales drove up the price of the primary illuminant and lubricant in the United States and Europe, causing, one might say, the world's first oil crisis. However, we must also agree that, after the discovery that previously known drilling techniques would work for oil and after the development of refining, whaling as a major industry was doomed.

But what can we conclude about the hypothesis that the increased scarcity of whales was an important, possibly the most important, cause of the rise of petroleum as a major industry? Well, we know that man had known about oil for centuries. People knew that oil burned and gave light many years before 1859. We also know that men were working on lamps to burn oil prior to that year. It was a relatively simple step to adapt existing lamps to facilitate the burning of refined petroleum, once the problem of odor was solved. Also, the methods used in coal oil refineries were easily adaptable to petroleum refining. The technology was already available in 1859, as evidenced by the rapid building of refineries in the Titusville area almost immediately after oil was struck.

Finally, the drilling techniques were well known. The drilling methods used for brine water were easily adaptable to petroleum. Bissell, who decided to drill for oil rather than dig for it, had absolutely no experience in drilling, but he must have known something about the process. As noted in *The American Petroleum Industry* (p. 81):

> As a driller, Drake was a rank amateur. At a time when it usually took only six to eight months to bore 1,000 feet or more through solid rock in the great salt fields along the Kanawha River, it took him two years to drill 69½ feet. When Drake finally reached his peak rate of 3 feet a day in August, 1859, he was boring at only about one-half the Kanawha rate of a decade earlier.

Nonetheless, Drake demonstrated that oil could be extracted from the ground at a substantial rate, just as Kier had earlier demonstrated that it could be refined in large quantities. But we must wonder: what if sperm whales had multiplied so prodigiously that whale oil remained at around 25 to 30 cents a gallon? Would people have been experimenting with petroleum refineries? With petroleum lamps? With methods to extract petroleum from the ground?

It's somewhat doubtful. And it would have been inefficient and wasteful to have done so. If whale oil had been 30 cents per gallon, few resources would have been expended to obtain petroleum. Whatever their contribution to mankind, the pioneers of the oil industry, Bissell, Kier, Ferris, Drake, Silliman, and their associates, were primarily, if not solely, interested in profits. Everything we read about the early days of the Pennsylvania (later the Seneca) Oil Company leads us to believe that the stockholders were mainly interested in turning a buck or two. They were continually arguing over money. There is strong reason to believe that if Drake had not struck oil when he did, or soon thereafter, the project would have been discontinued. Some of the stockholders did not even want to send him the last expense installment of $500. When the well hit, the company was really financially strapped. These men were profit seekers, not saints.

This is not to say that if the men of Seneca had abandoned the project others would not have struck oil soon. They would have. As evidenced by the onslaught of successful wells in the Titusville area after Drake struck oil, the technique was too simple to be delayed for very long. Certainly if Kier had not developed the first refinery, someone else would have. But the pioneers, as well as those who would have succeeded them had they quit or failed, were, or would have been, motivated by potential profits.

But would there have been these potential profits from innovation had whales remained plentiful and the price of whale oil low? Or what would potential profits from petroleum have been had whales become more plentiful and whale oil fallen in price? It doesn't appear likely that there would have been as great an incentive to drill for oil and experiment with refineries.

Certainly the petroleum pioneers were well aware of what was happening to the price of whale oil. From *Pennsylvania Petroleum* (p. 232), we quote William H. Abbott, who built the first refinery in the Titusville area. In a news story published in 1888 he wrote:

The first person to experiment with petroleum, and make a success at refining it, was Samuel M. Kier, of Pittsburgh. He procured his supply from the . . . wells at Tarentum. When refined he called it carbon oil. I purchased from him, paying $1.25 a gallon by the barrel. This was far superior to the oil made at that time in Canfield, Ohio, from the fine channel coal; or to whale oil which cost from $1.75 to $2.25 a gallon. It was a fortunate circumstance that on the decline of the whale-fisheries, and particularly, after the destruction of our whaling fleet by the rebels, during the last year of the war, there should be at hand so cheap and abundant a substitute; thereby preventing the public generally from suffering any inconvenience from the loss of whale oil.

Clearly, the introduction of petroleum was not simply a fortunate circumstance. The whale oil crisis and the potentially greater crisis were certainly ended by the emergence of petroleum. Certainly there is evidence that the pioneers of petroleum were strongly motivated by profits, and the high prices of whale oil pointed to potentially high profits in petroleum. No one sent them to the oil fields of Pennsylvania to benefit humanity or to alleviate suffering. They went to benefit themselves and in doing so benefited mankind.

On that note, we find it interesting to see what Ida M. Tarbell wrote in the introduction to *The Birth of the Oil Industry* (p. xxxix) in 1938:

It is certain, however, the development could never have gone on at anything like the speed that it did except under the American system of free opportunity. Men did not wait to ask if they might go into the Oil Region: they went. They did not ask how to put down a well: they quickly took the processes which other men had developed for other purposes and adapted them to their purpose. Each man made his contribution.

Taken as a whole, a truer exhibit of what must be expected of men working without other regulation than that they voluntarily give themselves is not to be found in our industrial history.

AN
ENGLISH
ENERGY
CRISIS
6

WHEN we described the timber crisis that occurred in America around the turn of the century, we mentioned in passing that Europeans thought Americans at that time were extremely wasteful of wood. And, by European standards, they were. We might ask why Europe had no wood problem in the early 1900s. Why were Europeans so conscious of wood conservation while America was so profligate? Why was there no timber crisis in Europe? Why did the technologies in the two continents differ so much?

The fact is that Europe had its own timber crisis about three centuries before America's. Europe responded to the crisis with a monumental technological change—a resource substitution so vast that, had it not taken place, there is good reason to believe that the Industrial Revolution would not have occurred.

In fact, Ester Boserup, in *Population and Technological Change* (p. 106), goes so far as to say:

> With increasing population density in Europe, shortages of wood became a major problem [in the late sixteenth century]. Many of the technology innovations in the eighteenth century were the

---

Much of this chapter is based on the work of John U. Nef in *The Rise of the British Coal Industry* and "An Early Energy Crisis and Its Consequences."

result of attempts to develop substitutes for wood for fuel and as raw material for industry and construction.

John U. Nef, the most eminent historian of the rise of the British coal industry, goes even further in his article "An Early Energy Crisis and Its Consequences" (p. 140):

> The first energy crisis [1540–1700], which has much to do with the crisis we now [1977] face, was a crisis of deforestation. The adoption of coal changed the economic history first of Britain, then of the rest of Europe and finally of the world. It led to the Industrial Revolution, which got under way in Britain in the last two decades of the 18th century. The substitution of coal for wood between 1550 and 1700 led to new methods of manufacturing, to the expansion of existing industries and to the exploitation of untapped natural resources.

This early natural resource crisis, which Nef calls simply "the timber crisis," must have been quite a problem at the time to have such far-reaching effects. Let's see why the crisis developed, how it was solved, and what problems arose. Even though the timber crisis occurred in most of Europe, we concentrate upon the timber crisis in Great Britain for three reasons. First, the crisis began in Britain; second, it was most serious there; and, third, the British were most successful in adapting to the problem.

THE GREAT TIMBER CRISIS

Before the 1540s, a timber shortage was far from people's minds as a problem to worry about. In "An Early Energy Crisis and Its Consequences" (p. 141), Nef points out that Vannoccio Biringuccio in *Pyrotechnia* (1540) wrote that the forests could fill all conceivable future demands for fuels, particularly for smelting.

> Miners are more likely to exaust the supply of ores than foresters the supply of the wood needed to smelt them. Very great forests are found everywhere, which makes one think that the ages of man would never consume them . . . especially since Nature, so very liberal, produces new ones every day.

According to Nef, coal is mentioned only once in the treatise *Pyrotech-nia:* "Besides trees, black stones that occur in many places, have the nature of true charcoal, [but] the abundance of trees makes [it] unnecessary to think of that faraway fuel" (ibid.).

But a revolution was beginning in Britain that would change it for centuries. This revolution would spread to most of Europe, and have far-reaching effects there. This was the Industrial Revolution.

However, before that revolution was accomplished, a timber crisis occurred in Britain. The crisis developed because foresters were depleting England and Scotland of their woods. Agriculture, industry, and commerce all contributed to the depletion. Furthermore, we should note that the British navy was putting large demands on wood—especially oak—for naval stores. In the seventeenth century, the strategic commodity in Britain was oak for warships. The reason for the rapid depletion was simple. From the middle of the sixteenth century to the end of the eighteenth, an amazing transformation took place in Britain. Over this period, the population roughly doubled, from three to six million. Over the same period, Britain became increasingly urbanized. In the 1530s, only one person in ten lived in a town. By the 1690s, one out of four was a townsman. London grew from a city of 60,000 to the largest city of Europe, with a population of 530,000.

The additional people required heat and housing, both of which required wood. In addition, the increased urbanization posed a special problem. The large concentration of people, especially in London, put a particularly severe strain on the forests near the towns and cities. As nearby forests were annihilated because of the building and heat requirements, wood had to be brought from farther and farther away. Since wood is bulky and not easily shipped, this increased distance substantially increased the price of wood in the towns.

The increase in population, combined with relative freedom from the religious and dynastic wars that so plagued the continent during this period, contributed to the great increase in British industrialization. The rapid increase in industrialization depleted the forests even faster, which in turn threatened to end the industrialization.

In the middle of the sixteenth century, wood—or charcoal that was made from wood—was a crucial ingredient in almost every manufacturing industry. Charcoal was used to smelt iron, tin, lead, and copper. Glass was becoming increasingly important in home construction, and charcoal was the fuel used in glass manufacturing. While the sun could be used on the continent for obtaining salt from seawater, in damp and chilly Britain this method of evaporation was not feasible. They had to use charcoal.

Brewing was a rapidly expanding industry at the time. Beer and ale had practically become the national drinks of Britain. Again, brewing required heat, and heat required charcoal. And, as we have noted, the British fleet was rapidly expanding. Ships were built of wood, further depleting the forests, particularly those in coastal areas.

So Britain was entering the Industrial Revolution, and the fuel that fired this revolution was wood. Wood was also the building material for the houses of the workers necessary to man this revolution. And it was the source of heat for their homes.

But the paradox was that the effect of the industrial expansion on wood prices threatened to end the expansion, because Britain was running out of its source of energy. As you would expect, the price of wood was driven up rapidly because of the heavy demand.

Let's take the price of firewood as an example. In Figure 8, we show price indexes in years for which data are available for firewood and general prices in Great Britain in the sixteenth and seventeenth centuries. The increases in firewood prices relative to the increases in general prices show how rapidly wood prices were increasing relative to other prices. It's easy to see how much more rapidly wood prices rose than the prices of goods in general. Over this period, the price of firewood rose 730 percent, but the general price index rose only 177 percent.

But the general index doesn't tell the whole story. The really severe pressure on the forests, and therefore on the price of wood, was around the rapidly growing urban areas, particularly London, where the industrialization was taking place. The problem was that industrialization couldn't take place without a nearby labor force, and people could not survive without wood. Yet industrial expansion and the rapid population increase in the towns were destroying the wood. So the problem was most acute where urbanization was occurring.

As Nef noted in *The Rise of the British Coal Industry*, "So rapid an increase in the cost of any commodity in common use must have been almost without precedent in the history of western civilization." Some of Nef's illustrations and references from the period vividly portray the growing crisis. For example, during the latter part of the sixteenth

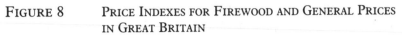

FIGURE 8   PRICE INDEXES FOR FIREWOOD AND GENERAL PRICES
              IN GREAT BRITAIN

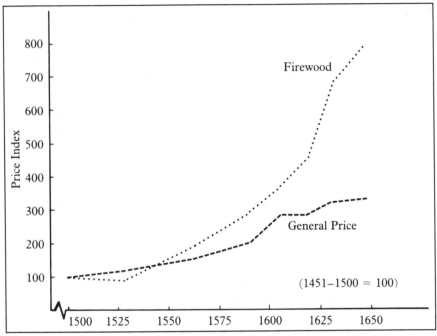

SOURCE: John U. Nef, *The Rise of the British Coal Industry*, p. 158.

century, dozens of commissions were sent by the Courts of the Exchequer of Queen Elizabeth and King James I to, quoting Nef, "investigate the spoil taking place in every county, and from every county came the same lament of deforestation."

Naturally, there was a clamor for intervention. Nef points out several examples. In 1585, the framers of a statute to solve the problem noted that the woods of Sussex, Surrey, and Kent had "been decayed and denuded [and] will in short time be utterly consumed and wasted if some convenient remedy therin be not timely provided."

Before that time, the London company of brewers had petitioned "that wood cannot be gotten to sarve all your . . . orators withoute the rewin and great decaie of the whole common Weale of the Citie." Orators without ale! A disaster.

A petition to Queen Elizabeth asking for export controls on wood stated, "all of the country villages round about the land within twentie myles of the sea are for the most part dryven to burne of theis coales, for that the most part of the woods are consumed." From Devonshire in 1610, "tymber for buyldinge and other necessiries for husbandrie are alreaddy growen soe extreame deare" that wood had to be imported. From Pembrokeshire, "this Countrie groneth with the generalle complainte of other countries of the decreasinge of wood."

From Cliveger in 1587, no wood was to be had "for divers miles . . . therabouts." According to a Crown survey in 1575, in Bamburgh, "great woods hathe been, but now utterly decayed and no wood at all remaineth thereon."

Scotland, if anything, felt the timber crisis even more than England. In 1621, "nomberis of thame bothe to burgh and land hes bene constrayned not onlie to cutt doun and distroy thair policie and planting, bot thair movable tymmer worke, to mak fyre of it . . . and in mony placies the trade of brewing and baiking for want of fyre is neglectit and cassen up."

By the second decade of the seventeenth century, England had begun to import timber, clearly at a great cost, since wood takes up a lot of space relative to its value. It is said that after the fire of 1666, London was rebuilt with wood from abroad.

Spurred by fears that the Royal Navy would not have the timber necessary for naval stores, Queen Elizabeth, near the end of her reign, attempted to reduce the depletion (and protect the Crown's own stock of a strategic resource) by prohibiting the use of wood from Crown forests without a special permit. Naturally, there was corruption. For example, the Countess of Rutland in 1584 complained to the Crown that wood promised her from Sherwood Forest had not been delivered. The Queen's minister, Burghly, noting the "great decaye and Spoile of wood within that Forest" and the fact that she had already received warrants for 420 trees for the repair of her castle and mills, replied that this was a large number of trees for the repair only of the castle and mills,

> especially wher as it hath bene informed unto me and Complained of that the greatest number of the said trees have not been imployed to the use they were allowed for but sold . . . for money and converted the same to the owners private use, which . . . is a verie foule disceit and abuse toward mee and wrong to hir Majes-

tie, which shall make mee more careful . . . and for the better preservation of the wood there I mynd to make a generall staye without uppon verie especiall occassion . . . pardon me that I write no more unto them therin then I have already donne but leave it to their owne good disrection, considering the state of the Forest and spoile already made. [Nef, pp. 160–61.]

So we have plenty of evidence that the energy outlook was gloomy. Also, while the shortage of wood occurred later on the continent, by the end of the seventeenth century the crisis had spread to most of Western Europe. Much of the wood was exhausted, and, like Britain during the entire seventeenth century, the rest of Europe was searching for a substitute. Two reasons the crisis occurred in Britain before it reached the continent were that the population was growing more rapidly in Britain and industrialization was developing earlier.

The rapid industrial growth in England and Scotland made great demands upon the available timber supply both for fuel and for building material. According to Nef, the success of the attempt at industrialization ultimately depended on the adoption of coal as fuel, and the necessity of substituting coal for wood at an earlier period than was found necessary in other countries had much to do with the powerful position that England had obtained among the nations of the world at the beginning of the eighteenth century. Her strength appears to have rested in some measure upon coal, a hundred years before the coal age is supposed to have begun.

THE AGE OF COAL BEGINS

Supposedly, the age of coal began in Britain during the early part of the eighteenth century; there was a huge increase in the use of coal during that century. However, Nef and other historians of the period date the beginning of the coal age from the middle of the sixteenth century, when wood started becoming increasingly scarce. Statistics certainly lend weight to the earlier date. Starting in 1550, spurred by the rapid rise in the price of wood, the use of coal as a fuel increased phenomenally.

For the 130 years from the decade 1551–1560 to 1681–1690, annual British coal production increased fourteen-fold, from 210,000 tons annually to 2,982,000 tons. By comparison, over the 100 years from the decade 1681–1690 to 1781–1790, the increase in annual production was much larger in terms of tonnage, to 10.3 million tons, but much less as a percentage—300 percent compared to the previous 1400 percent. By the latter part of the seventeenth century, coal was being used as a source of fuel in almost every industry in Britain, with the exception of iron smelting, in which all the technical problems involved in the adaptation had not yet been worked out. And these special problems were solved within the next few decades. Moreover, by the end of the seventeenth century, coal was the primary source of heat in most British homes.

Thus we have our familiar story. A country was running out of an important natural resource. In this case, wood. The rapid depletion, brought about by the huge increase in demand, caused the price of the resource to rise rapidly. In response to the resource shortage and consequent high prices, people undertook technological change and found a substitute that turned out to be preferred to the original resource at its new, higher price.

But in order to make this massive change in the source of fuel and energy, two difficult problems had to be solved. First, in industrial use, such as brewing, glassmaking, and especially in iron making, there was the problem of adapting the existing technology, which used wood and charcoal as the source of fuel, to a technology that used coal. The old wood-burning technology could not be used as it was. Modifications had to be made because the two fuels had great differences in their burning characteristics and certainly were not perfect substitutes, given the existing state of the arts in home use and in manufacturing. In some industries, firms were able to make the changeover with relative ease. In the iron industry, the new technology was not in widespread use until the eighteenth century. But, as we will show, even in that industry, in which the technological change came slowly, methods of wood conservation were developed long before the switch to coal was completed.

The second problem in changing from wood to coal was pollution, massive pollution. The use of coal resulted in the worst air pollution problem in history up to that time, possibly one of the worst ever. The reason was simple. Coal smoke stank; wood smoke didn't. Coal made the beer taste bad; wood didn't. Nef presents several examples of the problem.

A British "environmentalist" wrote a treatise in 1661 recommending removing all coal-burning artisans beyond Greenwich to rid London of the "Columns and Clouds of Smoake, which are belched forth from the sooty Throates of [those shops] . . . rendering [the city] in a few moments like the Picture of Troy sacked by the Greeks, or the approaches of Mount Hecla."

Another writer in 1729 noted that physicians made a practice of removing their patients from Dublin "out of the smoke of the city, which in winter is so thick, and cloudy enough to stifle men and beasts, so great an influence that it affects even the blossom and bloom of the flowers in the spring." (Environmentalists were certainly more articulate and colorful in those days.)

As early as 1307, the use of coal was forbidden to lime-burners in Southwark, near London. Included in the preamble to that proclamation is, "An intolerable smell difuses itself throughout the neighboring places and the air is greatly infected, to the annoyance of the magistrates, citizens and others there dwelling and to the injury of their bodily health."

And talk about strict environmental laws! As early as 1578, a brewer and dyer were committed to prison for burning coal in Westminster. Sixty years later, brewers near Whitehall could be sent to jail if they made free use of coal during the residence of the royal family.

Nef notes that sheer necessity alone could have forced the population to adopt a fuel regarded by many as not only disagreeable, but actually noxious. But, as Nef also says, "The substitution of coal for wood between 1550 and 1700 led to new methods of manufacturing, to the expansion of existing industries and to the exploration of untapped natural resources."

So let's take a look at how this massive technological change took place. We have already looked at the pollution problem associated with burning coal. But in addition, most products manufactured with open wood fires were damaged by coal fumes. Because of this problem, a considerable amount of innovation had to take place in the production processes in order to convert from the increasingly scarce wood to coal. New methods had to be found to protect the materials from the burning coal and the gases.

One of the first industries to make the change was glass manufacturing. This was an extremely important industry in Britain, which, because of its cold and damp climate, was more dependent on glass for its dwellings than were other areas on the continent. Glass manufacturers responded to the wood scarcity by developing furnaces with an arched roof to reflect the heat downward onto the materials to be heated, rather than upward. Also, the sand and potash were put in clay containers during the heating process to protect them from the coal fumes. This method of heating was later adapted to other types of manufacturing.

By 1618, the technology to make bricks using coal rather than wood as a fuel had been developed. And by 1640, coal was being used as a fuel by much of the brewing industry. This technological change in the brewing industry was quite difficult, because for a long time the fumes from burning coal ruined the taste of the beer and ale during the heating of the malt. Since brewing had expanded very rapidly in Britain during the sixteenth century, when beer and ale were becoming the national beverages, the ability to prevent the coal fumes from ruining the brew was not an inconsequential innovation as wood became more and more expensive.

An even more important wood-saving innovation, coming in the 1660s, was the adaptation of the reverberatory furnace for smelting nonferrous metals. This technological change permitted coal to be used in Britain to smelt lead, copper, and tin.

By 1700, the only metal that required wood for smelting was iron. There were major technological problems to overcome in adapting iron manufacture to coal. Some wood-saving changes were, however, undertaken during the seventeenth century in the production of pig and bar iron. One major change that occurred during this period was the movement of iron manufacturing from the cities, where, as we have mentioned, wood was most scarce, to rural areas where, because of much lower population densities, wood was more plentiful. In fact, iron manufacturers frequently moved from place to place during this period as wood was depleted. This simple but important adaptation to wood scarcity helped conserve wood to some extent in areas of greatest depletion.

Nonetheless, since iron was so important to Britain's industrialization, the search for a production process that used coal rather than wood as a fuel intensified as wood became a serious problem. While iron production in Britain increased substantially between 1540 and 1630, its growth was greatly slowed because of the wood shortage. Beginning in the 1620s, England had to rely considerably upon imported iron, primarily from Sweden. While the production of iron wares from pig iron increasingly used coal as a fuel, the production of pig iron from ore was dependent upon wood for heat. It was not until 1784 that a coal burning furnace could be widely used to produce wrought iron. At this time, Britain was able to begin another industrial revolution, a revolution made possible by its earlier coal revolution, which was itself a response to the earlier wood crisis.

1700—THE TIMBER CRISIS IS OVER

By the end of the sixteenth century, Britain, which was behind most of Europe in productivity during most of the Middle Ages, was the leading country in Europe in per capita agricultural and industrial production. With the exception of iron production, the vast majority of British industry had adapted to the high price of wood by developing the technology that enabled them to substitute coal for wood. Because of this massive change, they could compete favorably with products from the continent.

The brickmaking industry developed methods to reduce substantially the heavy breakage that occurred when coal was first used for baking bricks. This development, by reducing the relative price of bricks, led to substitution of bricks for wood in building construction, which further decreased the demand for wood. By 1700, the great majority of steaming and dying establishments in the textile industry—heavy users of fuel—used coal rather than wood as a fuel. Other manufacturing industries that converted extensively from wood to coal were food preservation, whiskey, brewing, soap, sugar refining, and fertilizer. In the case of fertilizer, Nef quotes a French visitor studying English technology in 1738–39 as saying that the new coal-burning kilns (made of coal-baked bricks) had produced such a superior lime fertilizer that the yield of arable land had tripled. The visitor considered coal "the soul of English manufacturers."

During the same period, British homes were continuously converting from wood to coal as a source of heat. Notwithstanding the smell, which was being remedied, coal was more efficient for heating homes, not an unimportant consequence in the cold, wet English climate. According to Nef in "An Early Energy Crisis and Its Consequences," in 1651 the author of *News from Newcastle* reported that sacks of coal had heightened the joys of intimacy. We will leave it to you to decide exactly what that author meant; but it is clear that the transition from wood to coal was treated as no small accomplishment.

By 1700, four times as much heating in homes and manufacturing was from coal than wood. By this time, the wood crisis was generally over. Wood prices, while still high, had leveled off. In fact, from 1660 to 1700 wood prices did not rise.

Nonetheless, other sectors of the British economy were still demanding wood, in spite of the great change from wood to coal for fuel and from wood to bricks and stone for construction. As we mentioned, the iron industry, because of technical problems, couldn't complete its change to coal until the 1780s. The rapid expansion of the British navy and merchant fleet still required increased amounts of wood.

But at the same time, Great Britain was stepping up its imports of lumber. Considerable amounts were being shipped from the American colonies and the Baltic countries. The majority of the imports were paid for with exports of manufactured goods like textiles, produced in very large part with coal as the primary fuel. Also, to substitute for the increased imports of wood, Britain, by 1700, was able to produce domestically many of the products it had previously imported.

Salt is a good example. Since fish was so important in the British diet at the time, salt was absolutely necessary as a preservative. During the first part of the sixteenth century, two-thirds of the salt used was imported, primarily from France, where sunlight was used to evaporate salt from seawater. This method was not feasible in the damp British climate, and wood heat was becoming too expensive as wood became more scarce. By 1700, using coal as a fuel for evaporation, Britain had become self-sufficient in salt production.

As you would expect, coal mining technology improved markedly during the conversion. The British came to realize that they were sitting on enormous coal deposits and better methods of mining had to be devised. For example, the development of the boring rod greatly aided the exploration of coal seams and enabled miners to evaluate the quality of deposits without sinking shafts. Pumping techniques to extract water from mines were improved, and new mining methods were devised.

In fact, it was in large part the need for increasingly efficient drainage systems in coal mines that led to the development of the steam engine. Likewise, a case can be made that the demand for cheaper, more efficient transportation of coal brought about the railroad. To go even further, quoting Nef (p. 148):

> The shift to fossil fuel in the 17th century led on after 1785 to the aggressive exploitation of the world's vast stores of iron ore. Without the coming of the first coal-burning economy the age of iron and steel might never have developed. The conversion to coal in Elizabethan England had further consequences in bringing into being the modern mechanized age.

So isn't it remarkable that the "age of coal," which had such far-reaching consequences for worldwide economic development, began on a relatively backward little island, primarily because that little island was running out of fuel? An energy crisis led to an era of growth and prosperity. But considering the other energy crises we have discussed, maybe it's not so remarkable.

AN ENERGY
CRISIS OF
ANOTHER SORT
7

I N the preceding chapter, we discussed a crisis that occurred imme-diately before the beginning of the period in history we call the Indus-trial Revolution. But what do we really mean by the term "Industrial Revolution"? Chiefly, we refer to the replacement of labor—human power—with machine power. In the nineteenth century, the ma-chines that replaced labor were powered by steam. If, however, we continue to use the definition of the replacement of labor power with machine power, we would say that a much earlier industrial revolution had already occurred—this earlier revolution was during the late Middle Ages. The only difference between the two revolutions is that the earlier machines were powered by water rather than by steam.

The late Middle Ages were characterized by a huge expansion in the use of water power to replace human labor. By the end of the fifteenth century, water power was widely used not only to grind grain but also in fulling textiles (i.e., matting and shrinking the woven cloth), forging, and papermaking. Whether or not you wish to call this an industrial revolution, most writers agree that the experience gained with water-powered machines was in large part responsible for the technological explosion of the nineteenth century. The transition from the water-powered machines to steam-powered machines was not very great. The techniques were similar; only the source of power was different.

We might ask, what led to this expansion in the use of water power during the Middle Ages? Why did it not occur earlier? The technology had existed for well over a thousand years. But, after reading this far, you probably expect us to assert that this substitution of machine power for labor was the result of an economic crisis; and you're right. In this instance, it was not a natural resource crisis but a labor crisis— a shortage of human energy—that was responsible for the technological change.

AN ANCIENT TECHNOLOGY

Before discussing the reasons for the labor crisis and the massive substitution of water power—machines—for human power in Europe during the late Middle Ages, let's take a look at the state of water technology at that time and see why water power had not been extensively used previously. It's clear that the use of water as a source of energy did not have to be invented in the Middle Ages. The technology of water power is very, very old. Probably waterwheels were first used in the last century before the Christian era—most likely in the Eastern Mediterranean. A Greek epigram from the Augustan Age depicts nymphs grinding corn using water power. Many ancient writers—including Pliny—document the existence of mill-wheels for grinding corn in the rivers of Italy. The first mill probably appeared in England about the middle of the ninth century. By the eleventh century, the first fulling mills (used in the production of textiles) were in operation, and we know (from the *Domesday Book* of 1086) that there were over five thousand such mills operating in England.

Thus, the technology for using water power was available and had been for a long time. However, it was not until the late Middle Ages— the fourteenth and fifteenth centuries—that the technology became widely used. Why wasn't it used more widely earlier?

If we look at the ancient world, the answer is clear: labor was abundant and therefore cheap. At the beginning of the Christian era, the world was heavily populated. As Marc Bloch wrote, "Rome . . . saw its streets seething with a hungry proletariat." If labor was cheap, why employ a technology that saves labor? Since the Romans had an enormous amount of cheap labor, they used this cheap labor rather than more expensive capital to grind the grain. Doesn't that sound familiar? When gasoline was cheap, did we try to find a technology that saved gasoline? When wood was cheap, did we try to conserve wood?

Moving to the early Middle Ages, we again find a surplus of labor. From 850 through 1347, the population in Europe increased steadily. As might be expected, the economic organization of production reflected this abundance of labor. More and more, labor was applied to the production process. This was particularly true in agriculture. Cultivation was labor-intensive. Human power was even cheaper than animal power. And, as should be expected, hand-operated mills were a familiar object throughout this period.

Hence, before the plagues struck Europe, the technology for water-powered machines was available but was not very widely used. The reason? An abundant supply of labor. There was simply no reason to adopt the labor-saving, capital-intensive technology when labor was cheap.

ONE HECK OF A WAY TO GET A WAGE INCREASE

The population growth in Europe ended tragically after the middle of the fourteenth century. In December of 1347, the Black Death swept into Europe and within three years the plague had struck the whole of Western Europe. In a very short period of time, the plague swept from Southern Europe throughout the entire continent.

In the years from 1348 to 1350, the Black Death—or as the Germans appropriately called it, "The Great Dying"—ravaged Europe. Eighty percent of those who contracted the plague died within three days. Between 35 and 65 percent of the population of Europe died! (For example, it is estimated that the Black Death reduced France's population from 17 to 10 million.)

Although the Black Death was the worst single plague to hit Europe, it was only the opening blow of three centuries of pestilence. In England, the long affliction was climaxed with an outbreak of bubonic plague in 1665. Moreover, in France from the mid-fourteenth to mid-seventeenth century, there are only nineteen years for which the records show no evidence of plague or pestilence.

Before we get to our basic argument, you might find it interesting to note how the people reacted to the Black Death and the various plagues that followed. According to the chroniclers of the period, people tended to have one of two kinds of reactions. One response was an increase in religious fervor. People would divest themselves of all their wordly goods and opt to lead a life of prayer and devotion. The other response—and, according to the chroniclers, the more common one—was to indulge in wordly pleasures as much as possible. If I am going to die tomorrow, why should I save today? Indeed, we find laments about this type of behavior contained in the writings of the social critics of that period.

Completely accurate population numbers for this period are impossible to obtain and different researchers present different estimates. However, to illustrate the magnitude of the population decline, consider the estimates in Table 4. The great decrease in population must have reduced the available labor force substantially. You can't reduce population that much without eliminating a vast number of workers. Such a reduction in workers has to have a tremendous impact upon the production process. And it did.

Once labor was no longer abundant, it was no longer cheap. As we have seen in the case of other inputs into the production process, when the supply of a productive input is reduced significantly, the users of that input bid against one another and drive up its price. This was certainly the case for labor in the fourteenth century. Every writer we have surveyed indicates that wages rose dramatically after 1350. With the decline in the availability of labor, the price of labor—i.e., the wage rate—had to rise, and rise it did. Perhaps the best characterization is provided in Figure 9. After the onset of the plague, wages rose

TABLE 4   THE IMPACT OF THE BLACK PLAGUE ON
             ESTIMATED POPULATIONS IN EUROPE
             (in millions)

	1300	1400	Percentage Decline
England	3.7	2.3	38
France	17.5	11.5	34
Germany	17.0	12.0	29
Italy	8.5	6.0	29

SOURCE: Daniel McGary, *Medieval History and Civilization*, p. 563.

FIGURE 9   REAL WAGES IN THE THIRTEENTH AND
            FOURTEENTH CENTURIES

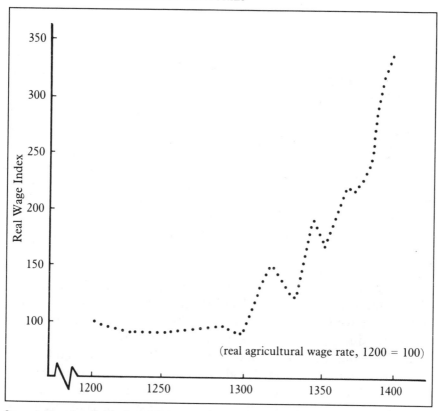

(real agricultural wage rate, 1200 = 100)

SOURCE: Douglass C. North and Robert Paul Thomas, *The Rise of the Western World*, p. 14.

substantially, while food prices—wheat prices—remained relatively stable. Thus real wages—wages in terms of the commodities that could be bought—rose dramatically during the fourteenth century. (The spike in wages that is evident prior to the arrival of the Black Plague is the result of a somewhat similar occurrence—the great famine of 1315–1319. Over this period, it is estimated that the death toll in England was as much as 20 percent of the population.)

Due to the plagues of the fourteenth century, Europe was faced with a human energy crisis. Labor, which had been abundant for the preceding five centuries, suddenly became very dear. As with our own "gasoline pestilence" of the 1970s, something had to give. Producers had to find a way to conserve the now scarce resource. They had to come up with a substitute.

HOW YA GONNA KEEP 'EM DOWN ON THE FARM?

To see the effect of this labor shortage, let's concentrate our attention on England. At the beginning of the fourteenth century, England was an agricultural nation. The typical prototypes of medieval society in this period were the knight and husbandman. More specifically, landowners concentrated on growing cereal grains using labor-intensive techniques. Landowners made almost no use of machines or even of animals. Labor plowed the fields, planted and cut the grain, and provided the power to grind it. The tools they used were primitive. Indeed, these tools were practically unchanged since the Roman era. Technology had remained unchanged for a thousand years. What need was there to develop a new technology when labor was so abundant and so cheap?

However, with the shortage of labor and the resulting increase in wages, such techniques were no longer economically feasible. The flight of the peasants from the land became common despite all efforts of the landowners to prevent it. As labor became more and more scarce, producers in the towns increasingly bid away labor from the farms. How did they do it? Quite simply by offering higher and higher wages. Put yourself in a medieval peasant's place. With rising wages, what would you do? We expect that you would do just what the peasants did then. The result was a mass exodus of labor from the farm to the city. Indeed, it was during this period that the geographic mobility of the peasants became possible, as traditional obligations of the peasant to the lord were effectively eliminated. The scarcity of labor led to a change in the social order of Europe. As Philip Ziegler put it in *The Black Death* (p. 293):

> The sudden disappearance of so high a proportion of the labour force meant that those who already worked for wages were able to demand an increase while those who had not yet achieved this status agitated to commute their services and share in the benefits enjoyed by freemen. If the landlord refused, conditions were peculiarly propitious for the villein [serf] to slip away and seek a more amenable master elsewhere.

In order to keep the peasants on the farm, the landowners had to pay higher wages, a response that was, to say the least, disagreeable to them.

As you would expect, the powerful landowners attempted to prevent this exodus and stop the rise in wages. In England, they were able to obtain laws that attempted to limit the increase in wages and restrict the mobility of labor in 1349, 1351, 1388, and 1406. But these were to no avail. The incentive to increase wages and bid away labor was just too great. With the decline in population, labor was just too valuable. Peasants continued to leave the farms for higher paying jobs in the towns. Wages remained high while land rents fell. It has been argued that while the peasants and artisans were better off in the post-plague era, the upper class—the landowners—suffered.

So, what did the landowners do? As labor became more expensive, some lords began to experiment with innovative, labor-saving agricultural techniques to replace those that had been used for centuries. Alternatively, many landowners converted their tilled fields to sheep pasture. That is, they substituted away from the labor-intensive grain crops to a land-intensive product, wool, since labor prices had risen and land prices had fallen. As you would expect, when more wool was produced, wool prices eventually fell.

Nevertheless, some landowners profited during the period of increasing wages. Harry Miskimin tells of Sir John Fastolf, who drew substantial revenues from clothworkers on his estates. The point is, though, that Sir John's success was the result of his location. His estates at Castle Combe had access to water power to drive the fulling mills. In contrast, the revenues of the Bishop of Durham had, by 1446, dropped to one-third of their 1308 level. Sir John apparently succeeded by switching from expensive labor power to relatively less expensive water power. The Bishop of Durham did not have the advantage of the swiftly-running streams to power the mill wheels.

So we see in agriculture a substitution of products and of an old (but previously unused) technology for human power. Sheep raising, which required relatively little labor, became increasingly common. And water powered the mills that helped to turn the wool into cloth. By replacing labor power with water power in the fulling process—until then the most labor-intensive process in the manufacture of cloth—England in particular was able to adapt to the labor crisis. Before the Black Death, England had been an importer of finished cloth (from the Flemish and the Italians); but after 1351, all evidence indicates that England became a net exporter of finished cloth.

The same story was apparently taking place in the towns, where wages were also rising. As labor became more expensive, producers attempted to find ways to make labor less essential. As in the case of agriculture, this technological change took the form of the substitution of less labor-intensive means of production; more significantly, it involved the replacement of labor power with machine power. Can we find other examples of this switch from human power to water-powered machines?

A MEDIEVAL MACHINE AGE

There exists substantial evidence that the period following 1350 was characterized by a widespread search for mechanical power. Perhaps the best known example is found in the *Notebooks* of Leonardo da Vinci (1452–1519). Evidence of the drive for more uses for water power are also found in the works of Agricola, Ramelli, and Zonca, who documented the changes that were being introduced. Many of the technological changes of this period involved the introduction of water-powered machinery.

But we must note that there were no substantial improvements made in the design of the water wheel itself during this period. The overshot wheel—where the water struck the top of the wheel—continued to be used. (Leonardo da Vinci's suggestions for a water turbine were not put in practice until the nineteenth century.) It was in the uses of water power that the substantial advances were made. As we mentioned earlier, water power was originally used to grind grain, but until the fourteenth century humans were almost exclusively the predominant source of power for grinding. As labor became expensive, water-powered machinery was extensively substituted in grain production. Such grain mills sprang up throughout Europe. Furthermore, during the late Middle Ages water power was adapted to all sorts of other uses.

As we have pointed out, one of the first applications of water-powered machinery was in the textile—wool—industry. Because wool was becoming more and more abundant and labor more and more expensive, it was only natural that manufacturers in this industry would turn to machine power.

According to the editors of *The Cambridge History of Europe*, by the fifteenth century "fulling mills crowded the valleys running up into the hills." Furthermore, by the fifteenth century, water power had been adapted to finishing cloth. Instead of the very labor-intensive process of drawing tassels over the cloth by hand, a water-powered "gigmill" had been adopted. Given this machine experience, is it any surprise that textiles became the leading growth industry in the Industrial Revolution of the nineteenth century?

Water power also began to be extensively used in mining. By the end of the fourteenth century, water wheels provided the power for the pumps that drained the mine shafts of water. It powered bellows to heat the ore and the hammers to crush the ore.

The use of water power to operate bellows and hammers was also expanded in the iron-making industry. Large water-powered bellows produced a much higher temperature in forges, permitting the production of much larger masses of metal. With the larger masses of metal, the water-powered hammers were adopted in order to reduce the metal to wrought iron. (Again, the step that was taken from water power to steam power in this industry in the nineteenth century was simply not very great.)

Hence, the evidence we have seen clearly suggests that there was an extensive expansion in the use of water power during the late Middle Ages. Although the technology of water power had been known for some fifteen hundred years, it was only after 1350 that the "[Water] Machine Age" began. The technology was essentially unchanged; but in the fifteenth century, Europeans were using water to power machinery much more than had the Greeks or Romans.

Why? If there was no technological breakthrough, why did the late Middle Ages see such an expansion in the use of water power? We feel that this switch from labor power to machine power resulted almost solely because of the labor crisis. With the onset of the plagues, a labor shortage resulted and led inevitably to a huge increase in the wage rate. As wages rose, producers searched for a production technology that would reduce the essentiality of labor. The result was the adoption of machine power—an industrial revolution in the Middle Ages.

In this account, we have dealt with labor rather than with inputs we more normally think of as natural resources. However, we believe there is little essential difference. With the shortage-induced increase in the price of any major input, users attempt to substitute away from the more expensive input. As we have already seen, it happened with oil in the 1970s, crude rubber in the 1920s, timber in the early 1900s, whale oil in the mid-nineteenth century, and charcoal in the seventeenth century. Is it then surprising that it happened for labor in the fourteenth century?

CRISES IN ANCIENT GREECE

8

WE in the West owe a great debt to the ancient Greeks and tend to stand in awe of this ancient civilization. Greek civilization has had a tremendous impact on our modern societies. In fact, we trace the origins of science to this culture and regard Greece as the cradle of our modern democracy.

Today, our view of this ancient civilization is clouded not only by time but also by Hollywood's romanticism. If you are like us, you probably have a view of ancient Greece as a very stable and secure society. Could economic crises have occurred in such an environment?

Of course they could occur; and they did. In this chapter, we will describe two important resource crises experienced by the ancient Greeks and show how they responded to the shortages. The first crisis we describe is another timber crisis, this one having a major impact on shipbuilding, occurring during the latter stages of the Byzantine empire. The other crisis, occurring during the very early period of Greek civilization, was a scarcity of tin that led to a massive shortage of bronze—the basic metal of the Greeks during that period. We will see that in the shipbuilding crisis, the Greeks responded with technological change. In the case of the bronze crisis they substituted an alternative commodity. In both cases, the response was elicited by shortage-induced price increases.

AN ANCIENT TIMBER CRISIS*

Let us begin our discussion with a question: How would you build a boat? Most of us would follow the plan shown in Figure 10. First we would lay a keel (1). Then we would attach a frame (or ribs) to the keel (2). Finally, we would attach the planking (or metal sheeting or fiberglass) around the frame to form the hull (3). Such a method of ship construction is obvious to us, because frame-first construction is the way that boats and ships have been constructed for as long as we can remember. It is certainly the logical way to build a boat.

FIGURE 10   FRAME-FIRST SHIP CONSTRUCTION

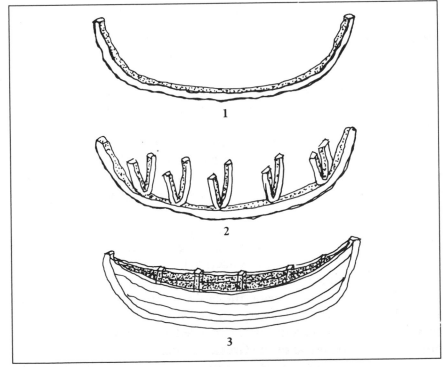

SOURCE: Public Broadcasting Associates, Inc., "The Ancient Mariners."

---

*Much of the discussion in this section is drawn from a program appearing on PBS—"The Ancient Mariners"—in the *Odyssey* series (Public Broadcasting Associates, Inc.)

However, that is not the way that ships have always been constructed. In 1967, a group of nautical archaeologists began excavation of a shipwreck off the north coast of Cyprus near the small town of Kyrenia. The remains of the ship, which had been sunk around 300 B.C., indicated that it had been constructed hull first. The shipwright had followed the pattern shown in Figure 11. He began by laying a keel (1). But then, instead of building a frame, he began building up the hull, plank by plank. Each plank was held to the next by mortise and tenon joints (2). In this way, the ancient shipwright "sculpted" the hull of the ship (3). Only after the hull was complete were frames added to strengthen the ship (4).

The Kyrenia wreck suggests that ancient ships were constructed in the hull-first method. This assertion is supported by the works of Homer. Lionel Casson has shown that the description of the building of Odysseus's boat implies hull-first construction. As related by Homer, once the goddess Calypso was ordered to send Odysseus on his way:

> He felled twenty trees in all and lopped
> Their branches, then skillfully hewed them and smoothed
>   them straight
> To the line. Meanwhile, the lovely Calypso brought augers
> And he bored and fitted all the pieces just right and joined
>   them
> With pegs driven through the lined-up holes . . .
>
> [*The Odyssey*, Book V, trans. by Ennis Rees.]

Many earlier translators erroneously concluded that Odysseus had constructed a raft. However, given what we know now, the passage makes more sense. He had built the hull first, boring and pegging and hammering the planks into place, inserting the framing only after the hull was complete. In short, Odysseus's ship was constructed in precisely the same manner as was the Kyrenia wreck. The hull-first method of shipbuilding was the method with which Homer must have been familiar.

So this must have been the way the ancient Greeks built their boats. And they must have built a great many of them, for the Greeks were a seafaring people. Many of their wars were fought predominantly on the sea. We must conclude that this technology was proba-

FIGURE 11   HULL-FIRST SHIP CONSTRUCTION

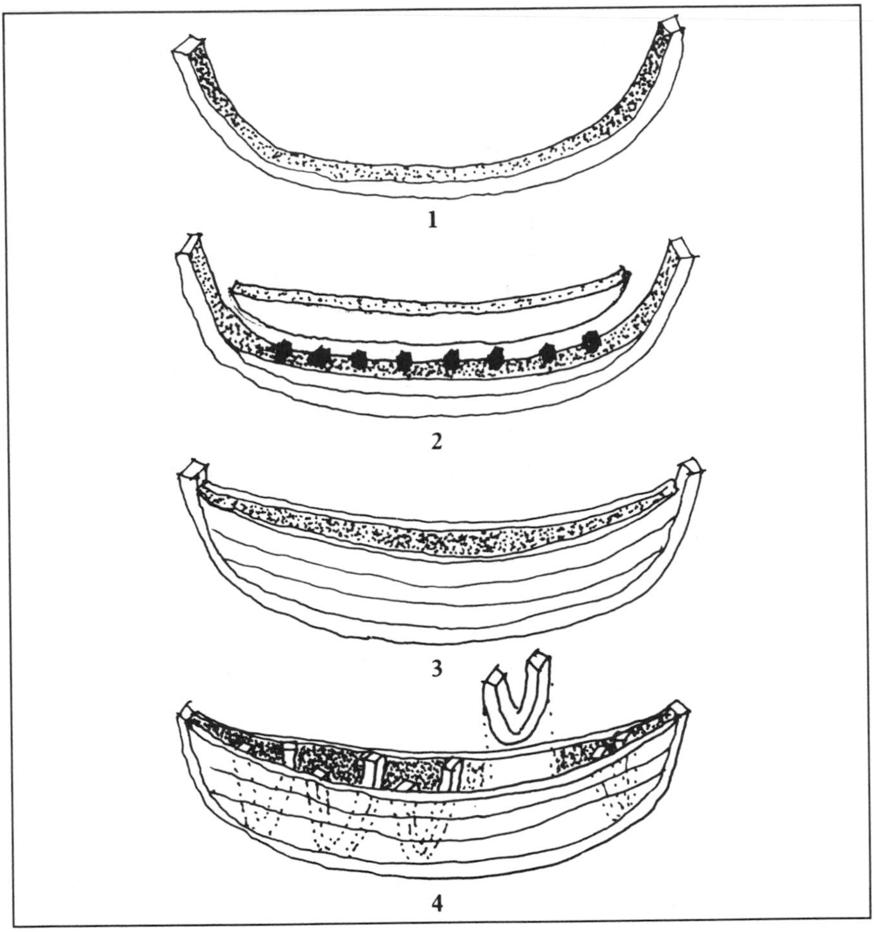

SOURCE: Public Broadcasting Associates, Inc., "The Ancient Mariners."

bly efficient for the time. And, as we shall see, this method of construction was used for a long, long time.

But we know that the Greeks did change from exclusive use of
hull-first construction to frame first. Let's try to date the transition in
construction techniques and find a reason for the change. Evidence
from the excavation of two other wrecked ships can help to provide
the answers.

Another wrecked ship was discovered near Serce Liman off the coast of Rhodes. Still another sunken Greek ship was found a little further north at Yassi Ada, off the coast of Turkey. Evidence shows that the Serce Liman wreck was a ship that last sailed in 1025 A.D. It was constructed in the modern frame-first manner. The other wrecked ship at Yassi Ada was dated much earlier, around 625 A.D.

The construction of this earlier wrecked ship combined the hull-first and frame-first techniques. From the keel, the bottom half of the hull was constructed in the hull-first method. The rest of the hull was constructed in the frame-first method. Hence, between 300 B.C. and 1025 A.D. we know that there was a revolution in shipbuilding techniques and we know further that the transition occurred around 625 A.D.

Where do we stand now? We know that there was a major change in shipbuilding technology and we know, within broad limits, when it occurred. But the crucial question is as yet unanswered—why did this technological innovation occur? What caused the ancient shipwrights to abandon the time-honored method of shipbuilding and adopt a new technology? It is with this question that we are primarily concerned.

To answer this question, let us reexamine the ancient hull-first construction. The ships used by the ancient Greeks were certainly not rafts or oversized rowboats. They were intricate works of art as well as functional vessels. Clearly, then, the planks that made up the hull of one of these ships had to make a lot of twists and curves from bow to stern. Since ancient shipwrights had no frames to bend the planks against, they had to cut a plank with precisely the required twists and curves from a solid log. They had to chop and scrape away at the log until they had a plank with just the shape required to fit into the hull. In the process, they had to cut away as much as 80 percent of the original log. The point is that hull-first construction was labor- and timber-intensive. This method required a lot of time and a lot of trees to construct a single ship.

On the other hand, with frame-first construction, several boards could be cut from a single log and these boards could be bent around the frame to form the hull. This modern technology would save a lot of labor and even more timber.

The preceding discussion suggests a solution, but we need to know more. Of course frame-first construction saves labor and timber. But if labor and timber were cheap, there would have been no reason to conserve them. We have already seen that when resources were cheap, people didn't conserve them. And they shouldn't have. Only if the price of one or both of these inputs were rising would the ancient shipwrights have wanted to conserve them. What can we say about these ancient prices?

Certainly a great decline in the use of slaves over this period may have contributed to an increase in the price of labor during the period. But because of the absence of statistics, we do not feel that we are on particularly firm ground when dealing with labor prices. We do, however, have some evidence about what was happening to timber during this period of transition. So we will concentrate on that input.

During the period in question—the seventh and eighth centuries—the Byzantine Empire and the Moslem Arabs (from what is now Saudi Arabia) were in conflict. Much of the conflict between these warring groups took the form of naval battles. Indeed, even by modern standards, we can say huge naval battles. For example, when the Moslems assaulted Constantinople in 718 A.D., the Moslem fleet alone was made up of 1800 ships. We are told that, of these, only five made it back to their home port in Syria. Certainly the Greeks were also using a lot of ships. Here then is the key. Both sides were sending huge fleets to sea and experiencing extremely heavy losses—due both to the warfare itself and to attacks by pirates. To replace these ships, more had to be built; so more trees had to be cut down. Experts generally agree that this contributed to the deforestation of the Mediterranean area; in short, the Greeks experienced a great timber shortage.

Once seen in this light, the story takes on a very familiar line. As more trees were cut and a shortage of timber was experienced, the price of timber rose. One way of looking at this increase in the price of timber is that more resources had to be expended to locate and transport the timber necessary to build a ship. How did the Greeks react? They reacted in precisely the same way America did when faced with a shortage of timber—they began to conserve the scarce resource. And they conserved it in their most wood-using industry. Greek shipbuilding in the seventh century was the American railroad industry of 1900. The ancient shipwrights adopted a new technology that would save the scarce and therefore expensive timber. In this instance, we see evidence of an induced technological change that is not so different from our own switch from eight-cylinder to four-cylinder automobile engines during the oil shortage.

THE END OF THE BRONZE AGE

Let's turn now to an even earlier crisis in ancient Greece. When we were in school, we remember our teachers characterizing man's history in terms of three ages—the Stone Age, the Bronze Age, and the Iron Age. While we will have something to say about scarcity in the Stone Age in our next chapter, we want now to look at the transition from Bronze to Iron. Specifically, why did our predecessors switch from bronze to iron tools and weapons? Certainly this transition represents a great advance in human history.

In the area that would become Greece, the initial transition occurred in approximately 1000 B.C. Ancient Greece appears to be one of the first places in which iron became a "working metal"—i.e., Greece was one of the first places in which iron was used other than for ornamentation. Hence, we will use Greece as our setting as we attempt to explain this revolution.

When confronted by the question of why the ancient Greeks switched from bronze to iron, most people we have asked have given us one of two basic responses: (1) the ancient Greeks did not know about iron (or did not discover how to make it) until 1000 B.C.; and (2) iron was a much better metal than bronze. Although they sound plausible, neither of these responses is correct.

Let's first address the assertion that the Greeks did not know how to make iron. There is strong evidence that they did in fact know how to make iron long before 1000 B.C. Iron was probably first produced in Asia Minor many centuries before—perhaps as early as 3000 B.C. But while iron was known, it was not widely used. People in ancient Greece had the capability for making iron long before they entered into the Iron Age.

The technology of making iron required three capabilities: (1) heating to a temperature of 1100°C; (2) carbonization; and (3) quenching—the sudden cooling that would harden the iron. There is strong reason to believe that the Greeks circa 1000 B.C. had all three.

First, the required temperature of 1100°C had already been achieved in the smelting of copper and bronze. So the Greeks certainly could have smelted iron ore using techniques developed for other metals. Second, the smiths who smelted the bronze had discovered long before that the carbon content of metal could be increased by using charcoal for fuel.

To provide some evidence that the Greeks knew that plunging hot metal into water rapidly cooled the metal and hence hardened it, we again turn to Homer. Remember that while the great epic poems were not written down until about three centuries later, historians agree that they were probably composed and recited before 1000 B.C. Thus, these poems would reflect the state of the art that existed prior to 1000 B.C. Homer describes Odysseus thrusting the red-hot olive stake into the eye of the Cyclops in the following manner:

> As when a worker
> In bronze dips a large ax or adze into cold water
> To temper it and a great hissing is heard—
> For iron at least is strengthened by dipping in water—
> Even so his eye hissed around the green olive pole.
>
> [*The Odyssey*, Book IX, trans. by Ennis Rees.]

It would appear then that the knowledge required to make iron was available prior to 1000 B.C. However, again referring to *The Odyssey*, remember that Odysseus and his men carried bronze weapons and used bronze tools. The Greeks conquered Troy with bronze weapons. If the Greeks had the technology to make iron, why didn't Achilles kill Hector with an iron sword? Why wasn't iron more widely used?

As we noted earlier, the other common response is that iron was vastly superior to bronze. However, our sources indicate that the hardness of hammered bronze is very close to that of early iron. Bronze weapons and tools were almost as hard and could hold an edge almost as well as iron. Iron did have the advantage of being lighter than bronze; but since the early smiths could not make large points or blades, this advantage was not very significant. Hence, we do not find any evidence of iron being vastly superior to bronze at the time.

Given then that neither of the obvious answers is valid, let's look more closely at the period in question. From trading records, we know that during the Bronze Age iron was extremely expensive. For example, trading records from the nineteenth century B.C. suggest that the exchange ratio for iron and silver was one iron to forty silver. During the Bronze Age, iron was so highly valued that there existed laws controlling its export. Indeed, its value can be illustrated with artifacts like a gold ring decorated with iron wire. In many regions of the ancient world, iron was so valuable it was used as money. Is it any surprise that no one was using iron as a working metal? When was the last time you used a gold bar as a hammer?

Although the preceding discussion explains why the Greeks were using bronze rather than iron, it clearly does not help to explain the switch to iron that occurred after 1000 B.C. To answer this question, let's begin with another question: What exactly is bronze? It is an alloy of copper and tin or copper and arsenic. For obvious reasons, the Greeks (as did most others) used copper and tin. Some copper was available in the Aegean, but the primary source of copper for the Greeks was Cyprus. We know that during the Bronze Age copper and silver were exchanged at a rate of approximately 200 copper to 1 silver. So copper was relatively cheap—especially compared to iron. (Remember, 1 iron was worth 40 silver.) Tin, on the other hand, was not as abundant. There was no tin in Greece and practically none in the entire eastern Mediterranean area. Therefore, the Greeks had to trade with other nations to obtain tin. While the precise source of the tin is uncertain, it is likely that it came from Persia (Iran). During the Bronze Age, the exchange ratio for tin and silver was between four and ten units of tin to one unit of silver. So during this period tin was more expensive than copper; but the price of tin was not even in the neighborhood of that for iron. Since bronze contained 10 percent tin, we could say that during the Bronze Age the components for a bronze tool cost about five one-hundredths of 1 percent (0.0005) of what an iron tool would have cost.

Clearly, if circumstances had remained the same, the Greeks would have never switched to iron. (Indeed, we might complain about bronzing a shirt rather than ironing it). However, circumstances did change.

Since Greece allowed free trade, there were no government controls on metal prices. The price of copper or iron or tin varied with availability. And, about 1000 B.C., tin became almost nonexistent in the Aegean. The Greeks experienced a tin crisis of monumental proportions.

What caused the tin shortage? We know that all communication and trade in the Aegean were disrupted between 1025 and 950 B.C. For this period, there exists no evidence of any traded items. That is, the archaeological record indicates that there was no trade taking place. Greece was isolated. The cause of this disruption in trade has been traced to the invasion of the "sea peoples" (for example, the Philistines and the Dorians) into the eastern Mediterranean. Indeed, it was this invasion that led to the collapse of the major Bronze Age civilizations—the Hittite Empire, Mycenaean Greece, and New Kingdom Egypt. The eastern Mediterranean experienced social chaos. Trade was no longer possible; and as we noted earlier, without trade Greece had no tin. Additional evidence of the tin shortage was found in a shipwreck in Cape Chelidonia. This wreck, dated in the late thirteenth century B.C., contained a load of bronze scrap that was to have been melted down for its tin content.

With tin no longer available, bronze was no longer cheap. The shortage of tin raised its price and thereby the price of bronze. As the price of bronze rose, iron became a more attractive substitute. While tin was not available in the Aegean, iron ore was. Indeed, iron ore is spread liberally over the earth's surface. Thus the rising price of bronze induced the ancient smiths to begin using iron. The age of iron had begun.

With the virtual elimination of tin supplies, the ancient Greeks began to use iron as a working metal. No longer was iron considered to be a precious metal to be used only for ornamentation. Although iron was still expensive, its price had dropped relative to bronze.

However, we do not want to give you the idea that the Greeks completely stopped using bronze. It was, after all, the metal with which they had the most experience. It was the traditional resource. Indeed, once trade was reestablished in the Aegean, bronze prices dropped; so we would expect many users to revert to bronze. Bronze continued to be used for several more centuries. For example, we know that the Battle of Marathon in the fifth century B.C. was fought with bronze weapons. But—and this is the critical point—iron had made an inroad. The experience with iron would not be forgotten.

This Greek experience is not all unlike our own recent experience with petroleum. During the energy crisis, the shortage of gasoline forced us to switch to small, fuel-efficient automobiles. Today we see consumers demanding larger automobiles and more performance. As the Greeks reverted to bronze, we are reverting to traditional vehicles. But does this mean that we will return to driving the gas guzzlers of the 1960s? Certainly not! The cars we drive today—even the largest of the currently available models—are much smaller and more fuel efficent than those of two decades ago.

In the same way, the Greek's return to bronze was not complete. Even after the price of bronze declined toward its previous level, iron continued to be used. And as the smiths worked more and more with iron, the experience they gained enabled them to make it more cheaply. Indeed, we know that by the seventh century B.C. the price of iron relative to silver was 2,000 iron to 1 silver. Think about that for a moment. We saw that in the Bronze Age the iron:silver exchange ratio was 1:40. This later exchange ratio is 2,000:1. That is simply a massive decline in price. The price that existed in the seventh century was equal to 1/80,000 of that which prevailed during the Bronze Age.

The ancient Greeks switched from bronze to iron because a resource shortage—a tin crisis—raised the price of bronze. They substituted a new product for the one that had become scarce. And once they gained experience with the new product, they found ways of reducing the cost of production. Hence, competition reduced its price. In this way, the Greeks moved out of the Bronze Age into the Age of Iron.

What can that experience nearly 3,000 years ago teach us? How does it relate to our own situation? Alternative energy sources like solar energy have been known for decades, but we have not made use of them. Why not? With cheap petroleum available, it was simply not feasible to use the alternative sources. Solar energy was too expensive. However, what can we expect if the price of petroleum rises? We propose that what we can expect is precisely what happened in the case we have just described; the alternative energy sources would become more attractive substitutes. And with a vastly superior technology, the transition would be much more rapid. If the price of crude oil and natural gas rises high enough, people will begin to adopt the new product. And as producers gain experience with the new product its cost will fall. It is important to remember that the ancient Greeks switched from bronze to iron not because of some government edict but rather because of the rising price of bronze relative to that of iron. The same situation could be expected in energy or any other resource. No governmental intervention would be necessary. The Greeks' experience—particularly the decline in price of the new product—justifies an optimistic view of our own future.

CRISES IN PREHISTORY
9

THROUGHOUT this book, we have argued that resource shortages—or resource crises—have been quite common in the course of
human history. The recent oil crisis is not unique. So far, we have
dealt with critical shortages that have been described (at least partially) in written records. If we are to delve further back into mankind's history we are forced to abandon the written record and resort
to archaeological evidence. Since we feel it is essential to demonstrate
that conservation, substitution, and technological innovation are the
natural reactions of man, we will take that step and begin to explore
the behavior of primitive man in response to resource shortages.

As you might expect, it is somewhat difficult to find evidence of
the prevailing economic conditions in the physical artifacts left by
primitive man. However, we feel that we have located two instances
that illustrate the way man has reacted, and always will react, to
resource shortages. The first might be viewed as an anecdote, relating
the behavior of more primitive peoples to our own behavior during the
recent energy crisis. The second, we feel, is more significant. We
assert that the transition of man from a food collector to a food
grower—perhaps the most important revolution in the history of

We are particularly grateful to Prof. Harry J. Shafer (Anthropology Program, Texas
A&M University) for his help in defining the topics that are discussed in this chapter.

man—was in response to a resource shortage. With this basic outline in mind, let us proceed.

RECYCLING IN THE STONE AGE

In the 1970s, the word "guzzler" took on a very specific meaning. The word itself brings to mind an automobile that gets poor gasoline mileage. Those of us who drive larger automobiles are sometimes hesitant to admit it for fear of being labeled as a gas guzzler. Indeed, we Americans have gone so far as to beat our collective breast and lament how we "wasted" gasoline and oil during the 1960s. However, as we demonstrated in the first chapter, the real reason Americans drove cars with poor gasoline mileage and lived in poorly insulated houses during the 1960s was because gasoline and other petroleum fuels were cheap. Quite simply, we reacted to the low price of the commodity by consuming more of it. When the price of gasoline began to rise in the 1970s, our reaction was to move to more energy efficient automobiles and houses; we switched from being guzzlers to conservers. Moreover, there was a move toward recycling goods that used a lot of energy in their production. An excellent example is aluminum. In the 1960s, we discarded our aluminum cans because it was cheap to make more aluminum. However, when the price of energy rose and new aluminum became much more expensive, we began to collect and recycle our cans—a process requiring substantially less electric energy (but more human energy) than the processing of new aluminum from bauxite.

We Americans changed from guzzlers to conservers and recyclers because energy became more expensive. Is this reaction unique to Americans or to so-called modern societies? Our survey of history indicates that it definitely is not. We have, in the preceding chapters, presented some more modern evidence of this behavior. But it is our assertion that all people—including primitive peoples—consume more of a good if it is cheap and consume less and resort to recycling if the good is expensive.

To provide some evidence bearing on this assertion, we will use an example drawn from a Stone Age people. Specifically, we use evidence from the artifacts deposited at two Mayan villages that were located in what is now northern Belize. While the date associated with these villages is fairly recent—approximately 300 B.C.—two things should be stressed. First, we are dealing with a Stone Age civilization. That is, flint tools and weapons were the norm. Although metallurgy was developed in the Mediterranean as early as 5000 B.C., metals were not in use in the Americas until the first centuries A.D. Second, our conversations with anthropologists and archaeologists indicate that the situation we describe is not unique; other sites provide similar evidence from earlier civilizations. We use this particular evidence simply because we have the advantage of personal contact with some of the researchers actively involved in the excavation.

The two sites we will describe are known as Colha and Kokeal, the latter located at an area known as Pulltrouser Swamp. In the discussion that follows, remember that we are dealing with two villages occupied by members of the same population and located only 20 miles apart.

Let us look first at Colha. This village was located in a region in which flint was very abundant. Indeed, along a creek that flows through the site, one can still find large flint nodules measuring up to a meter across and almost half as thick. Flint was plentiful, so it was cheap in terms of the effort required to get it. (By this, we mean that the people living at Colha had to expend very few resources in order to obtain flint.) How did the people who lived in Colha react? Quite simply, they "guzzled" flint. Put yourself in their place for a moment. Suppose you broke a spear point or a tool. What would you do? With flint so plentiful, why not discard the broken implement and make a new one? This is precisely what the archaeological record left in the form of the lithic artifacts indicates. Archaeologists working at Colha found large points and tools or else once-broken implements. There was almost no evidence of reworking to repair a broken implement. The archaeological evidence indicates that the philosophy of Colha was to use then discard. Why not? With an abundance of flint, why would they conserve it?

In the Pulltrouser Swamp region, the people were farming using an elaborate system of raised fields surrounded by irrigation ditches. (Quite a feat in itself; but we will have more to say about agriculture later.) More to the point, however, there were almost no flint deposits in the immediate region and the few that existed were of relatively poor quality. Flint was scarce, so it was expensive—the people living at Kokeal had to expend more resources in order to obtain flint. How then did these people react? Let's go back to the hypothetical question we asked at Colha. Suppose a spear point or tool was broken. What would you do? Given that flint was scarce, you would have to repair the broken implement. The broken point could be reworked into a smaller but still usable point. In other words, the implement could be recycled. The archaeological record deposited at Kokeal indicates that this is exactly what happened. Researchers have unearthed almost none of the large implements characteristic of Colha. Instead, the artifacts discovered were much smaller and exhibited evidence that they had been reworked from larger implements.

These implements found at Kokeal also showed substantial re-touching—the edges had been resharpened. Thus, Kokeal provides evidence of recycling in the Stone Age. If an implement was dulled, it was resharpened. If an implement was broken, it was recycled into a smaller, but usable, implement. Even more, the small fragments of flint found exhibited patterns of wear. What does this imply? The small fragments of flint from a broken tool or point were not dis-carded but were collected, sharpened, and mounted in a handle to be used as tools, like scrapers. In the region of Pulltrouser Swamp, flint was expensive so the peoples of that region were conservers and recyclers.

As you might expect, the flint artifacts found at Kokeal were originally obtained from Colha. Thus, we are actually talking about the same type of flint in both areas. However, in Colha flint was cheap, while in Kokeal it was expensive. The resultant distribution of artifacts is illustrated in Figure 12. In Colha, the researchers found both the blanks (left side) and artifacts in their pristine condition (center). At the Pulltrouser Swamp site researchers discovered the recycled artifacts (right side).

To summarize, where flint was abundant the people "wasted" flint. When an implement was broken, it was discarded. Where flint was scarce, it was conserved and recycled. When an implement was broken, it was reshaped or made into another implement.

Think about it for a moment. These people at Kokeal were Stone Age people. They weren't modern era or Victorian era Englishmen or Americans. They weren't even sophisticated Athenians from the golden age of Greece. Their culture was primitive in comparison. Yet they didn't need modern man or an intertemporal peace corps to tell them what to do. They had no Drive Slowly, Save Gas billboards—or billboards saying Be Careful With Your Spear, Save Flint—to remind

FIGURE 12   ARTIFACTS DISCOVERED AT COLHA AND KOKEAL

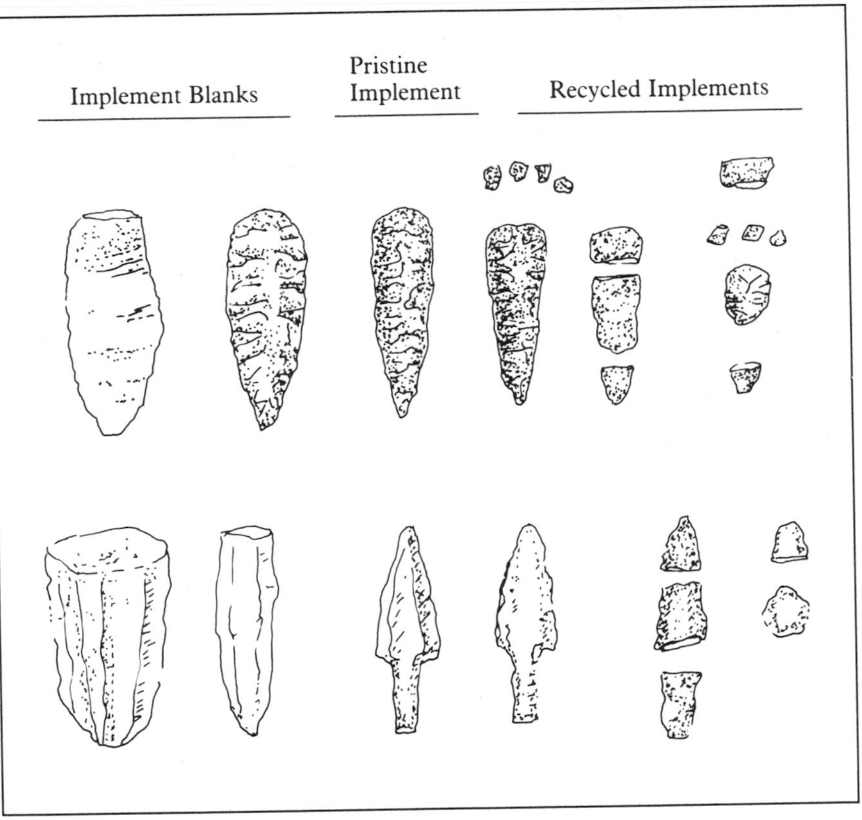

SOURCE: B.L. Turner II et al., "Maya Raised–Field Agriculture and Settlement at Pulltrouser Swamp, Northern Belize," p. F-40.

them to conserve. There were no TV commercials admonishing them to save flint.

Why should modern man be any different? Look at our most recent crisis. We behaved in the same way. When gasoline was abundant—cheap—we "guzzled" gasoline. Once gasoline became scarce—expensive—we conserved gasoline and recycled commodities that used a lot of this scarce energy. The behavior is the same; only the commodity in question is different. When a commodity is cheap, people consume a lot of it. Only when a commodity becomes expensive will people turn to conservation and recycling.

THE FIRST AGRARIAN REVOLUTION

Let's turn now to another resource crisis in prehistorical times. This is possibly the most important crisis of all. In earlier parts of this book we argued that scarcities—crises—have been responsible for many of the major "revolutions" in the evolution of modern societies. As you will remember, we discussed instances like the change from labor power to (water driven) machine power in the Middle Ages and the transition from the Bronze Age to the Iron Age.

We now turn to one of the most significant revolutions in the history of mankind—the change of man from a hunter-gatherer to a food grower. This change ranks with man's mastery of fire as a requirement for the evolution of society as we know it today. Once primitive man changed from a nomadic hunter-gatherer to a food producer, the stage was set for the growth of villages, towns, and cities. Indeed, some researchers have argued that, had this revolution not taken place, the maximum population of the world would be only 20–30 million. As some of the population began to specialize in the production of food, others were released to specialize in other pursuits—manufacture, trade, or the arts. We owe today's diverse society to this change that occurred some ten thousand years ago.

Our objective then is to determine what led to this revolution. While there exist competing explanations, our reading of the works of researchers in this area has convinced us that the transition from food gatherer to food producer was the result of a scarcity not entirely unlike later crises we have examined. Put another way, we feel that this first agrarian revolution was the result of an economic crisis in prehistory.

Before we began our research, we had a view of the primitive hunter-gatherer as living constantly on the verge of starvation. According to this traditional view, primitive man was constantly on the move, scrounging a bare subsistence from a harsh land. Obviously, if this were true, one could explain the transition to food production simply as the change to an easier means of obtaining nourishment. However, recent research simply casts serious doubt on this explanation. For example, many anthropologists point to the present-day Kung bushmen living in the Kalahari desert in southern Africa. Although these people have a level of technical competence that is inferior to that of many groups of people in the prehistoric era, they are able to obtain sufficient nourishment with less than three days of foraging per week! And this evidence was collected during a long drought in the area. The fact that this is possible in a desert area, in the middle of a drought, for a people using an inferior technology suggests that primitive man living in the lusher environments in the prehistoric era would have done even better. Indeed, the available evidence indicates that the primitive hunter-gatherer would have had not only adequate supplies of food but also more leisure time than do modern-day industrial or farm workers.

It would appear then that growing food was certainly not easier or less time consuming than gathering it; so the transition to food production cannot be explained simply as the move to an easier method of obtaining food. Put yourself in their place for a moment. Would you willingly undertake the labor of growing food and tending animals if sufficient food were available for the taking? We would not. Indeed, those of us who spend our days in factories and offices might wish to return to the leisurely existence of the primitive hunter-gatherer. What then would explain the transition? It had to be a crisis situation. Something must have occurred to raise the cost of gathering food sufficiently to make growing it a viable alternative.

To support our crisis view, we rely on the work of Lewis Binford, who pointed out that the apparently idyllic existence of the primitive hunter-gatherer was predicated on the population remaining stable at a density below the carrying capacity of the environment. As long as this equilibrium was maintained, there was no reason for mankind to change its behavior. In economic terms, if the population was below the carrying capacity of the environment, the cost of collecting food was less than that of growing food; so man would obviously opt to be a gatherer. However, when this equilibrium was disrupted—i.e., when the population exceeded the carrying capacity of the environment— primitive man faced a crisis, in this case a food crisis. When this happened, mankind either had to adapt or starve. Luckily for us, mankind adapted by becoming food producers.

According to Binford, the crisis could have arisen from either of two sources: (1) the physical environment could have changed so as to reduce the availability of plants and animals; or (2) demographic patterns could have changed so as to increase the population. Although Binford stresses the latter, there exists evidence that both of these types of disturbances preceded the introduction of agriculture in prehistory. Let's look at some of the available evidence.

With respect to environmental conditions, this era—approximately 8000 B.C.—was primarily influenced by glacial movements. As the glaciers advanced or retreated, climate was altered; so the plants and animals in a particular area probably changed. For example, in what is now France, the retreat of the glaciers changed the physical environment from plains that were rich in game to forests. Kent Flannery has argued that similar changes occurred in the prehistoric Near East. Such climatic changes would clearly affect the cost of food gathering to the population living in the area, since the availability of plants and animals was affected. Faced with these changing conditions, man would have to adapt. One such adaptation was an increase in the exploitation of fish, shellfish, and wild fowl that many researchers assert was in response to the disappearance of large mammals. The primary point is, however, that changing environmental conditions did alter the availability of food and did therefore change the cost of food gathering relative to food production. Primitive man responded to this change in precisely the same way that we did when faced with changes in the relative prices of heating oil and insulation—he opted for the method that involved a smaller expenditure.

The other source of a food crisis in prehistory—and the most significant source in Binford's view—was a change in demographic patterns. Something happened so as to increase the population in many areas to a level exceeding the carrying capacity of the environment. What was this something? In a closed society, it could be a change that either increased the birth rate or decreased the mortality rate. In an open society, increased immigration could raise the population above carrying capacity.

Following Binford, let's concentrate on the latter case. Suppose there was a group of primitive people living in what might be referred to as a "natural habitat zone." If this group maintained its population at a stable level, the individuals could have experienced a Garden of Eden existence, simply collecting their food requirements with a minimum expenditure of labor. If population remained stable, there would be no reason to turn to agriculture.

Now, suppose immigration into this area occurs. New people take up residence in the frontier area of the environment. We would certainly think the intrusion of immigrant groups would disturb the equilibrium that had previously existed. The environment could not support the increased population on the basis of hunting and gathering only. In short, a food crisis would occur. In such a case, we would expect agriculture to arise; but an interesting question involves the locus for the origins of agriculture. Where would we find the earliest forms? To answer this question, let us employ the following, very simplified diagram (Figure 13). We began with the original group of people—the native population—living in the most hospitable, most fertile area. Since the natives would protect their rights to the natural habitat zone, the immigrants would be forced to reside in the frontier area. Where then would we expect agriculture to begin?

Put yourself in the place of the original residents. Why should you change the way you do things simply because those outsiders showed up? Do you substitute a system of agriculture that involves hard work in order to feed the increased population or do you simply try to exclude the newcomers from hunting and gathering in the lusher area? To save your self-image, let us note simply that most societies opted for the latter approach. Hence, the origins of agriculture would be found on the frontier. In the frontier, the best lands for farming or herding would be those adjacent to the natural habitat zone—the land closer to the natural habitat zone would be more fertile than land

FIGURE 13   EXPECTED LOCUS OF ORIGINS OF AGRICULTURE

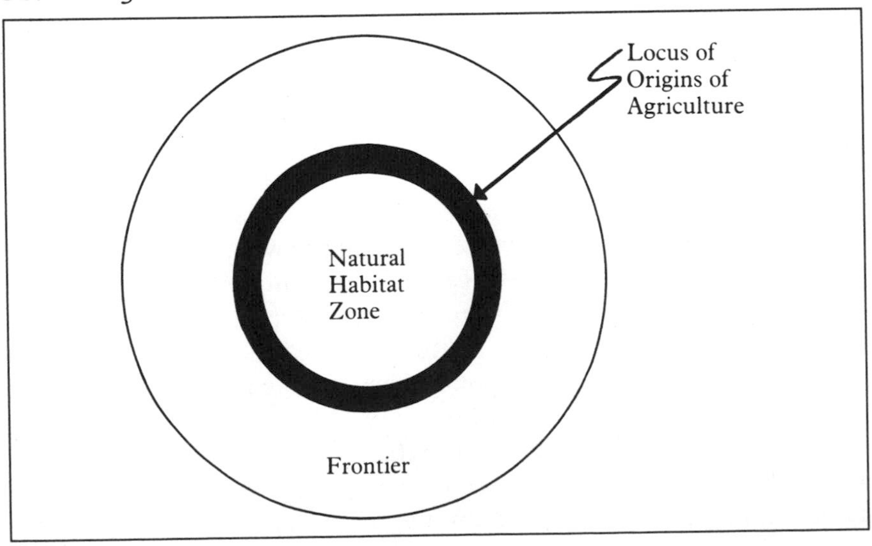

further out on the frontier. Therefore, if the preceding assertions are valid, we would expect to find the origins of agriculture at the edge of previously settled areas. That is precisely what the archaeological record suggests! Let's look at the early farming of food grains—wheat and barley in the Old World and maize in the New World. It turns out that the earliest records of agriculture are found in areas that are adjacent to areas that were already settled by populations that depended in large part on aquatic resources. (Cases in point are Natufian in the Near East and the coastal settlements of Mexico and Peru.)

Permit us to take a moment to summarize and restate the major points discussed in this section. We assert that the introduction of agriculture—one of the most significant revolutions in the development of modern society—was *not* the result of some slow, ongoing process. Life as a hunter-gatherer was easy, so why change? Instead, we assert that this revolution was the result of a crisis in prehistory. Something had to change to make the price of hunting and gathering food more expensive in terms of the time spent. We suggest that the change was an increase in the population relative to the carrying capacity of the environment and that this could have come about due either to climatic or demographic changes. Both of these conclusions are supported by the archaeological record. When the price of collected food rose (i.e., naturally occurring food in the environment became scarce) primitive man reacted with a change in technology and this technological change was the introduction of agriculture. The pattern through which agriculture developed certainly lends support to this thesis.

If we compare this to later experiences with resource shortages, we find that nothing major has changed in ten thousand years. As long as food was plentiful, there was no reason for primitive man to abandon tried and true methods in favor of new and sophisticated techniques required by farming and herding. Only when food became expensive was this new technology exploited.

THE NEXT CRISIS?

10

I N the preceding chapters, we have described ten economic crises experienced by man over the past ten thousand years. They illustrate what we feel are the two most important points concerning economic crises.

First, economic crises—or periods of scarcity—are more common than unique in the history of mankind. Crises have occurred due to a cut off of external supplies or, more simply, the depletion of a resource. If we have had shortages in the past, can't we expect more in the future?

Second, if people are allowed to pursue their own self-interest, the price of the resource will increase and the shortage will be eliminated. In our examples, we have seen that shortage-induced price increases have led to substitution away from the scarce commodity and/or to technological change. Since this has happened many times over the past ten thousand years, we fully expect that it can and will happen in the future.

Hence, we feel that economics is indeed an optimistic science. While we expect to confront more economic crises in the future, we are certain that if markets are permitted to function, these crises will be eliminated.

We do not purport to have a completely clear crystal ball; but it appears to us that there are several areas in which we might experience shortages over the next few decades. In the next two sections, we look at a couple of these potential crises and suggest what we feel might be the outcome.

ANOTHER ENERGY CRISIS?

In our first chapter, we argued that the energy crisis is over. And in the sense of massive shortages, long gasoline lines, and sudden price increases, it is. We base this projection not on our own crystal ball (or computer printouts) but rather on the actual behavior of the guys shooting craps for billions of dollars in Detroit and Houston. These billion-dollar crap games are played with oil, not dice. Based on what the major automobile and oil companies are doing, they must agree that another energy crisis is not imminent.

For example, in January of 1982, General Motors featured the new Chevrolet Camaro on the cover of its annual report, even before it was introduced. The Camaro and its Pontiac counterpart, Firebird, became GM's success stories for 1982. Both cars are sleek and sporty. And, equipped with eight-cylinder engines, both achieved a very unspectacular 15–17 miles per gallon. General Motors could hardly keep their dealers supplied. Certain Firebird models were at times in such short supply that some dealers charged above the window price—the first instance of a sticker price premium since the fuel efficient Hondas were introduced several years before. Seeing GM's success, Ford planned to introduce and feature a similar type of car in its 1983 Thunderbird. This doesn't sound as though GM and Ford are worried about $3.00 per gallon gasoline in the next few years. Put yourself in their position for a moment. If you expected a dramatic increase in the price of gasoline, would you be producing eight-cylinder engines? We certainly would not. If we predicted either a massive increase in the price of gasoline or shortages and long gasoline lines, we would opt for four-cylinder engine automobiles that were very miserly with gasoline.

Furthermore, according to the *Wall Street Journal* of January 22, 1982, Detroit was reviewing some of its muscle-car era designs. Ford was beginning production of a new "high output" four-cylinder engine for its subcompacts. It features two air scoops to feed into a bigger carburetor and a tubular exhaust/header for each cylinder. What is the purpose of the hood scoop? It forces more air down the carburetor, so more gasoline has to be fed in. If Detroit expected gasoline prices to increase substantially, would the hood scoops have returned? We assert that you can get Detroit's forecast for future energy prices by simply looking at the cars they produce. Are the hood scoops on or off? The fact that the hood scoops are reappearing tells us about the automobile makers' forecast for the price and availability of gasoline in the near future.

The automobile companies spend millions on advertising. What has been happening to their ads recently? What we see is increasing emphasis on performance and vastly decreased attention to gasoline mileage. Again, this would not be the policy of companies that expected rapidly rising gasoline prices, or long gasoline lines. For example, in 1982 Dodge featured its new Charger as your first chance to buy a "hot" car since the "hemi-head" Charger of the late 1960s. In auto ads, we see much more about 0–60 and much less about miles per gallon. Next time you see a car ad, notice the size of the type used to give the Environmental Protection Agency (EPA) mileage numbers. (Either those letters are getting smaller or our eyes are getting worse.)

What do the major oil companies think? Well, judging by what they are doing with their supertankers, they seem to feel that Americans will rely more and more on domestic production and less and less on Middle East oil. During the first four months of 1982, 35 very large crude carriers were scrapped (compared to 38 scrapped in all of 1981). Exxon recently sold five supertankers for scrap at $3 to $4 million each. It would cost $90 million each to replace those ships. Obviously, Exxon doesn't think the demand for Middle Eastern oil is going to increase. Indeed, more than 100 supertankers are laid up in foreign ports waiting for the scrapper's torch. The gasoline lines of 1973 and 1974 were the direct result of our dependence on foreign crude supplies. It would appear to us that Exxon expects that dependence to continue to decline and for the long gasoline lines to fade to a bitter memory.

So what can we conclude? Some say the glut in oil is temporary and that prices will once again increase dramatically as they did in the 1970s. But considering the actions of those who have the greatest incentive to be right about the future of energy, we must conclude that another decade of panic like the 1970s is unlikely.

However, as we noted at the end of the first chapter, in a broader sense—or over a longer period of time—there still may exist an energy crisis. It is getting harder and more expensive to find and extract crude oil. In order to get the producers to provide more oil in the future, higher prices will be required. So it is possible that over future decades the price of petroleum might rise steadily.

But given our experiences of the past, such a future should not be faced with gloom. This scenario is not at all unlike the situation we described with timber in the early 1900s, whale oil in the 1850s and 1860s, charcoal in the 1600s, timber in ancient Greece, and available food in 8000 B.C. In all of these cases, the resource became more scarce and its price increased. Given past experience, what can we expect in the future? Past crises did not end in collapse. Should we expect a collapse in the future?

If petroleum gets more scarce and the price of crude oil does rise in the future, past experience tells us that the market will react in two ways—with substitution and with technical change. With respect to substitution, traditional petroleum supplies can be made less essential in two ways. One way is for consumers to substitute other inputs for energy. We saw much of this kind of behavior in the late 1970s and early 1980s. Consumers switched from gas guzzlers to more fuel efficient automobiles, homeowners added insulation, and business firms searched for ways to reduce energy consumption. As the *Washington Post* reported on March 13, 1983, even during a period of falling oil prices, "oil users are still looking for ways to cut energy consumption." Since they have seen the massive increases in the price of energy that occurred in the past, consumers recognize that it could happen again in the future and they want to be ready. If the price of crude does rise in the future, it appears that oil users stand ready to adjust. As a result of price-induced substitution, oil is already much less essential than it was in the past. In 1982, it took 26 percent less oil to produce $1 of GNP—the value of final goods and services—than it did in 1973. And experiences of the past indicate that if the price rises in the future, petroleum will become even less essential.

The other way price-induced substitution can make oil less essential is for consumers to be induced to substitute away from expensive petroleum to other energy sources. One ready illustration is shale oil. We know it is available, but we do not now extract and use it. Why not? It is simply too expensive relative to traditional petroleum. But if the price of traditionally extracted crude rises, we would expect consumers to substitute this alternative energy source for the more traditional sources in the same way we once substituted petroleum for whale oil and the Greeks substituted iron for bronze.

With respect to technology, the range of potential change is extremely broad. However, the experience with crude rubber indicates that the development of a truly synthetic rubber was spurred by the high price of natural rubber. As a result of the development of synthetic, our consumption of natural rubber has declined to less than 5 percent of our total rubber consumption. While the current price of oil is below that which would make truly synthetic fuels economically feasible, there is currently a considerable amount of research aimed at true synthetic fuels. For example, a colleague of ours at Texas A&M University recently announced the development of a process that would permit the extraction of hydrogen fuels from water using only the power of the sun. Although such projects are still far away from commercial use, if the price of petroleum were to rise, these projects would gain impetus. Indeed, it is not impossible that one day the use of natural petroleum might be as rare as the use of natural rubber is today. (Thinking along these lines for a moment presents an interesting possibility. Saudi Arabia has consistently held OPEC to smaller price increases than those suggested by Iran and Libya. There is clearly a pro-Western tilt in Saudi Arabia's foreign policy; but, is there at least one other possibility? Given Saudi Arabia's large reserves, might it not be possible that Saudi Arabia is holding the price of crude down in order to delay the search for a synthetic?)

The upshot is that we are optimistic about America's energy future both in the near term and in the long run—as long as the free market is permitted to function. As we showed in our first chapter, it was government regulation—a suspension of the marketplace—that led to the crisis of the 1970s. Deregulation eliminated the crisis and we fully expect that, if the market is permitted to function, any future shortages will be eliminated via price-induced substitution and/or technical change. However, if government reinvolves itself in the energy market, it is completely possible that we could experience another decade of panic like (or worse than) the 1970s.

WATER—THE ESSENTIAL RESOURCE

With the decline in concern about energy, we have begun to hear more and more about an impending crisis that is potentially much more devastating. The following headlines show how Americans are being told that they are running out of water:

"A GRIM FUTURE FOR THE WATER-SHORT WEST"
Business Week, May 23, 1977

"IS U.S. RUNNING OUT OF WATER?"
U.S. News and World Report, July 18, 1977

"CRISIS OVER ENERGY COULD BE MATCHED BY
WATER SHORTAGES"
Wall Street Journal, June 8, 1978

"THE WATER CRISIS: IT'S ALMOST HERE"
Forbes, August 20, 1979

"WHAT TO DO WHEN THE WELL RUNS DRY"
Science, November 14, 1980

"THE BROWNING OF AMERICA"
Newsweek Special Report, February 23, 1981

"ARE WE HEADED FOR ANOTHER 'DUST BOWL'?"
Reader's Digest, May 1981

"WATER: WILL WE HAVE ENOUGH TO GO AROUND?"
U.S. News and World Report cover story, June 29, 1981

"WATER, WATER, RUNNING OUT"
The Nation, June 12, 1982

Don't these headlines look a lot like those we saw concerning energy? However, this similarity shouldn't be surprising. As we have demonstrated, all of the resource crises have much in common. It might be that the newspapers and magazines simply reuse old crisis headlines, changing only the resources—in this case, from energy to water.

The reports of an impending water crisis do, however, have a particularly dismal tone. In this instance, the prophets of doom remind us that we humans cannot exist without water. Their predictions of collapse seem even more self-evident than those we heard concerning the energy crisis—if we run out of water, we die. As exemplified in the *Newsweek* story, the doom merchants point to a bleak future: "In stately Greenwich Conn., . . . suburban matrons guard water like Bedouins and town officials lay plans for slit-trench latrines against the not-too-distant day when the reservoirs may run dry."

In the 1977 *U.S. News and World Report* story, we hear the experts predicting depletion—in the same way that other experts predicted the depletion of our oil reserves: "By the year 2000, only three of the 18 federally designated water regions on the U.S. mainland [see Figure 14] . . . will be able to live comfortably with their water supplies."

If these experts are correct, many of the rest of us are in big trouble. A particularly troublesome area is the important agricultural region watered by the Ogallala aquifer, a vast underground reservoir, extending 160,000 square miles under eight states. Illustrated in Figure 15, this section of "the great American desert" accounts for nearly 12 percent of America's cotton, grain sorghum, and wheat; and almost one-half of our beef cattle are fattened here. Now, *Time* reports in its issue of May 10, 1982, the prediction of a Boston engineering firm that "5.1 million acres of irrigated land (an area the size of Massachusetts) . . . will dry up by the year 2020."

How do these doom merchants reach their dismal conclusions? As you have probably guessed, they arrive at their forecasts in the same way the petroleum experts predicted the exhaustion of petroleum reserves in the 1970s and Malthus predicted a future of continuing famine in the late eighteenth century: they extrapolate from historical

FIGURE 14   EXPECTED AREAS OF WATER SHORTAGE BY THE YEAR 2000

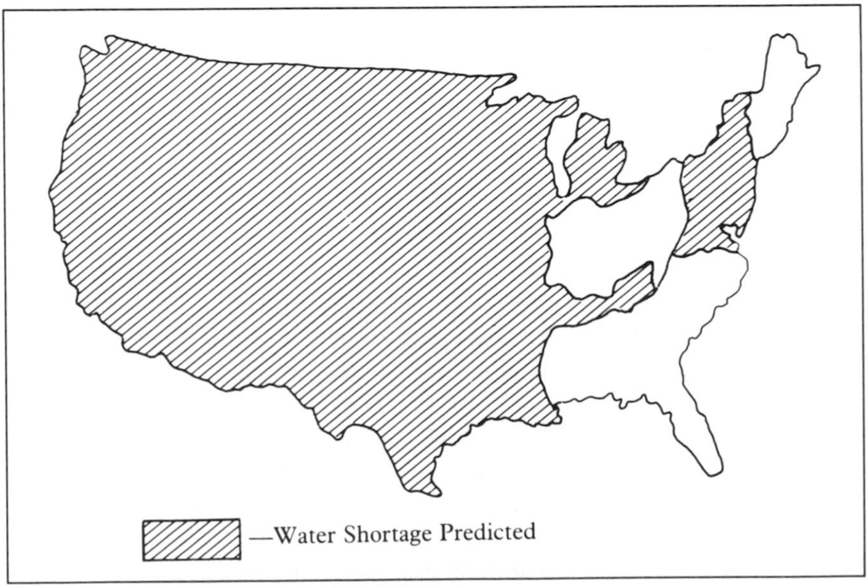

—Water Shortage Predicted

SOURCE: *U.S. News and World Report,* July 18, 1977, p. 34.

FIGURE 15   OGALLALA AQUIFER

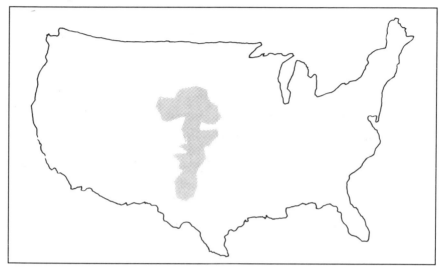

SOURCE: F.J. Heimes and R.R. Luckey, p. 3.

trends. If the growth in the rate of water use continues to follow the prevailing trend, then . . .

Throughout this book, we have argued that extrapolative forecasts are useless. Prevailing trends in the use of any resource—oil, timber, bronze, or water—have always and will always be altered by changes in the price of the resource. As a resource becomes scarce and its price rises, consumption will decline. Consumers will react with substitution and technical change. It happened for petroleum and all of the other resources we have discussed, and today it is happening for water. To show you precisely what is happening, let's look at the Ogallala Aquifer—the one experts believe will be depleted in 20 to 40 years.

The Ogallala Aquifer was first tapped in the 1930s. It was, however, the invention of the deep well turbine pump following World War II that transformed the face of our American desert. These high capacity pumps made irrigation feasible—i.e., the advent of the new pumps lowered the cost of raising the water from underground—and transformed the region from dry-land farming into an intensive farming economy based on irrigated feedgrains, cotton, and wheat. In

1949, less than one-tenth of the cropland was irrigated. This portion rose to one-sixth by 1959, to one-third in 1969, and to one-half by 1974. Over the last three decades, the number of water wells in the area increased from 2,000 to over 70,000.

The increase in irrigation certainly suggests that we might well pump out all of the water in this aquifer. The fact that the water was cheap induced the farmers to use a lot of it. What then happened to the stock of water contained in the aquifer? Since large-scale irrigation has existed longer in Texas than in any other state watered by the Ogallala Aquifer, let's look at what happened there. In the 1930s, it was estimated that in the portion of the aquifer underlying Texas there were some 485 million acre feet. (An acre foot is the amount of water that would cover one acre to a depth of one foot). By 1980, it was estimated that the remaining deposit held some 375 million acre feet—a reduction of 23 percent. If this rate of extraction were to continue, the doom merchants would be right—we would exhaust the Ogallala.

But as in all the other crises we have discussed, conditions changed. As more and more water was extracted, the price of water increased. In the 1970s and 1980s, the cost of extracting water from this aquifer increased radically. The first reason for this increase in cost is the simple fact that as more of the water was pumped out of the aquifer, farmers had to drill deeper and lift further to get any additional water. The water table in the Ogallala Aquifer has generally declined and the decline in the water table is most pronounced in Texas. In one Texas county, the water table has dropped by more than 150 feet since the 1940s. In 1948, only 15.5 percent of the wells in Texas were at depths of 150 feet or more. By 1977, over 90 percent of the wells were at this depth. As the water table dropped, it became more expensive to extract the water.

A second reason for the increased cost of water for irrigation was the rise in energy prices experienced in the 1970s. Energy costs make up a huge proportion of the total cost of irrigation. So with the increase in the price of energy, it became much more expensive for farmers to run the pumps to lift the water to the surface.

These two factors—falling water tables and increased energy prices—increased the cost of water to the users. How then did the users react? Like consumers of all the resources we discussed in earlier chapters, consumers of water reacted to the price increase by reducing consumption. The increase in price led to substitution and technical change. To see how this occurred, let's look at the techniques employed in agriculture in the High Plains of Texas since the 1940s.

At first, farmers used a simple, open-ditch system of irrigation, flooding the furrows. This system was not, however, very satisfactory for the sandy soil of the High Plains, since it was hard to get the water where you wanted it. The problem was, of course, that the water seeped into the soil so fast that it was difficult to move the water over any substantial distance. Hence, in the 1950s, aluminum pipe sprinkler systems were introduced. By 1962, 96 percent of the irrigated acreage was under sprinklers.

The problem with the early sprinkler systems was that they were very labor intensive. The pipes had to be moved and reconnected for each set of the irrigation system. As labor costs rose, more and more farmers moved to the center pivot system. By the mid-1960s, these systems, composed of a pipe that moves around a center pivot spraying a large circular area, became widely accepted. It was this technology that was being used as we moved into the 1970s and it is this system that results in those circular fields you can see from an airplane. An average system was equipped with 42 spray nozzles and could irrigate a quarter section (160 acres) on a seven-day schedule. This technology led the doom merchants to predict the exhaustion of the aquifer. They saw a system composed of large spray arms throwing water over a field, with much of the water evaporating in the process, and assumed that this method would continue into the future. They failed to consider the effect of price on water usage.

With the dramatic increase in the price of energy in 1973, the farmers in the region immediately began to search for ways to conserve this more expensive irrigation water. In the short run, they improved the nozzles used to spray the water onto the fields and began looking at lower pressure systems. In 1973, the Bureau of Reclamation found that, because the price of extracting water had risen from $3 per acre foot to $10 per acre foot, the efficiency in the use of water jumped from less than 44 percent to more than 60 percent. As the price of water rose, farmers used it more efficiently.

On a long-term basis, the users of Ogallala Aquifer water have begun to take additional steps to conserve this more expensive water. In tilling the soil, farmers are turning to furrow diking, a technique of building miniature dams in the furrows. This technique holds natural precipitation in place, giving it time to soak in rather than run off. By more effectively using natural precipitation, the farmers are less dependent on irrigation. In 1979, only 850,000 acres in Texas were furrow diked. By 1981, this had risen to 3.2 million acres. The users of the water are substituting natural precipitation for the increasingly scarce water from the aquifer.

Agricultural researchers have begun to experiment with chemicals that can reduce a plant's need for water. Growth regulators have been developed for cotton that not only reduce water requirements but also have increased yields by as much as 15 percent. Research continues on chemicals that reduce the evapo-transpiration rates of plants (i.e., the rate at which water is lost by the plant). In this area, technology has been used to substitute chemicals for water.

With respect to the irrigation system itself, farmers are beginning to turn to drip irrigation. Using a system of buried pipes, this system distributes small amounts of water directly to the roots of the plants. It has been estimated that the amount of water needed with such a system is only one-sixth of that required by a traditional sprinkler system and one one-hundredth of that required by an open-ditch system. As you might expect, these drip irrigation systems are expensive. In *Fortune* (February 23, 1981), it was estimated that the capital cost of a drip system is $1,000 per acre. Only when the price of water rises does it make sense to use these more capital-intensive irrigation systems. If the price of water were low, would you spend a lot of money to save water? In the case of water—as in all the other instances—an increase in its price has led the users to adopt new technology in order to reduce their dependence on the scarce, and thereby expensive, resource.

We could give other examples, such as switching from water-intensive to less water-intensive crops and the use of lasers to allow for more precise contouring of the field, to illustrate our point. As the price of water rose, farmers in the region of the Ogallala Aquifer reacted by consuming less water. This price-induced conservation was accomplished through substitution and new technology. Water is not unlike any of the other resources we have considered—if the price rises, the users will consume less of it.

The net effect is that water use from the Ogallala Aquifer is *not* continuing according to historical trend. Through the 1960s, the water table had been declining at a rate of from 2 to 5 feet per year. The doom merchants observed this trend and then predicted that if the rate of drawdown continued, we would quickly exhaust the aquifer. However, this rate of decline did not continue. In the 1970s, the rate of decline in the water table had been slowed to 1.42 feet per year. It would appear then that doomsday for the Ogallala Aquifer has been averted.

While we feel very optimistic about the future for water in the United States, we would be remiss if we failed to mention two problems we see in the case of water. Our optimism is based on the ability of the marketplace to ration a scarce resource. Hence, the problems we see are conditions that hinder the market from being able to perform this rationing function.

The first problem is one that has arisen before. Remember the elimination of rubber trees in South America and the rapid decline in the whale population that we described earlier? Why did these events occur? The answer is simple—no one owned the resource. If no one owns a resource and controls its use, the resource will always be overutilized. It happened with rubber trees and whales. It explains why the buffalo disappeared from the American West. It also explains why states impose bag limits on deer but none on cattle. In some instances, the same problem exists with water.

Consider a lake that borders on several different farms (or cities). How should each of the individual farmers behave? Each knows that the amount of water is limited; so should each farmer conserve? Certainly not. If one farmer were voluntarily to conserve, the others could extract all of the water. Hence, each farmer has the incentive to extract water as rapidly as possible in order to make sure that someone else doesn't get his share. Water would be extracted too rapidly.

What's the problem? As with the rubber trees in South America, whales, buffalo, and deer, no one owns the resource. No individual owns the water, so all of the users are induced to overuse the water (i.e., extract it too rapidly). Put another way, the price of water is too low. To each farmer, the price of a unit of water is only the cost of extracting it. Since no one owns the resource, no one considers the additional cost associated with that unit of water not being available for another use. And, as we have seen before, if a commodity is cheap, consumers will use more of it.

So the problem as we see it is to ensure that the price actually reflects the total cost of extracting and using the water. If this is done, the market can again perform its allocative function. With a higher price, the farmers would have an incentive to conserve, to use water efficiently. While there are several ways to accomplish this, perhaps the simplest and politically most expedient would be to impose a system of severance taxes on the water.

The second problem we see is allied to the first, but the solution is more straightforward. In many areas—most particularly the Midwest and Southwest—the buying and selling of water is restricted by the state. Let us give you a hypothetical example to illustrate these restrictions and their impact. Suppose you own a farm in one of the Midwestern states. With this farm, you also own the rights to some water, either from a river or from an aquifer. The restriction means that you cannot sell your water to someone else. What is the effect? Since you cannot sell any surplus water, your incentive would be to use it wantonly. That is, water would be used inefficiently—water would be wasted.

If, however, you were allowed to sell water, the price of water would rise, moving toward its replacement cost. (A *Fortune* article [February 23, 1981] asserted that the replacement cost—a number that more accurately reflects the true user cost—of water is 50 times what farmers are currently paying for it.) Obviously, as the price of water rose, the farmers would be induced to use the water more efficiently.

Hence, our solution to this second problem is simple: we propose that all restrictions on the buying and selling of water be removed. In this way, the marketplace would be permitted to ration the scarce water resource. Water would be employed in its highest valued use. No longer would we have someone wasting water simply because he or she could not sell the surplus to someone who doesn't have enough. We see a recent Supreme Court decision as a step in the right direction. A Mr. Joy Sporhause and his son-in-law, Delmer Moss, owned farms across the border from each other in Nebraska and Colorado and were using surplus water from their Nebraska land to irrigate their Colorado farm. They were moving water from a low-value use to a high-value use. The State of Nebraska determined that this transfer of water was illegal. That is, the state prohibited an implicit sale of water. Mr. Sporhause and Mr. Moss contested the restriction in the courts. In July 1982, the Supreme Court of the United States ruled in *Sporhause and Moss v. Nebraska* that the transfer of water was legal. This decision is a step in the direction of permitting a free market to exist for water. And we assert that if a freely functioning marketplace exists, we need not worry about a water crisis.

In general, we are very optimistic about the future for water. As we noted above, if the market is permitted to function we see no impending water crisis. It is important to note that our optimism is not based on government involvement. Indeed, we want to see governmental restrictions removed. One thing we certainly do not want is the establishment of a Department of Water. This view is certainly not universally held. Writing in *The Nation* of June 12, 1982, Fred Powledge made a plea for more governmental involvement. According to him, "government, so far, has been an abject failure at recognizing the water crisis, planning for it, protecting its citizens against it, informing them of it or figuring out what to do about it."

Mr. Powledge definitely wants government to do something. Among other things, he apparently wants government to somehow coerce us into conserving water by measures such as "not flushing a toilet" and "taking a plastic bucket into the shower with you to catch the runoff." We adamantly oppose such an idea. Notwithstanding the enormous enforcement costs of such policies, we think they are simply unnecessary. In a free market, if water is scarce its price will rise and consumers will conserve automatically. We need only to look at our experience in the 1970s to see this demonstrated. All of the crises we have told you about were solved by the market, not by government. Our assertion is then that government involvement is not necessary. We do not want the government to "do something." Indeed, given our experience with price controls on petroleum in the 1970s, we are afraid that government involvement is the very thing that changes a normal shortage into a crisis. It is with this issue, the advisability of government intervention, that our final chapter will be concerned.

A DOOMSDAY IN OUR FUTURE?

11

W E hope that by now you have been infected with our optimism. We believe that, if the marketplace is allowed to function, it will allocate scarce resources and thereby eliminate any future resource crises. A functioning marketplace will avert the resource-based Armageddon that some self-styled experts have predicted. As we told you at the outset, our faith in the marketplace is based on a simple observation: markets have dealt successfully with resource shortages for the past ten thousand years! We see no reason to expect this market system to suddenly fail today—as long as it is not suspended as it was during the 1970s.

In a market economy, if a resource shortage arises, the price of that resource will rise. On this point, even our friends the doom merchants agree. However, the point that they have failed to incorporate into their analyses is that the price increase induces changes in the behavior of the consumers and suppliers of the scarce resource. As we first demonstrated in our discussion of the energy crisis of the 1970s, if the price of the resource rises, consumers will conserve it, either directly as did the flint users or, more likely, by substituting other commodities for the now more expensive scarce resource. We saw this kind of behavior in the railroads' use of timber at the turn of this century, the switch from whale oil to petroleum in the nineteenth century, and the switch from human power to water power following the plagues in Europe. Furthermore, the rising price will induce the consumers and suppliers to resort to new technologies to make the scarce resource less essential. In the stories we related to you, we saw this behavior occur in the development of synthetic rubber, the rise of iron technology in ancient Greece, and even the introduction of agriculture in 8000 B.C. Together these price-induced changes in behavior—substitution and technical change—alter those trends from which the doom merchants predict collapse. If price is permitted to perform its allocative function, resource shortages will continue to be eliminated, as they have in the past.

Note, however, that our optimism is predicated on the marketplace being permitted to function. Our stories have indicated to us that it was simply the actions of individual consumers and producers—responding in accordance with their own self-interest—that eliminated the crises of the past. It was the participants in the marketplace—not government— who negated the prophecies of doom.

"WE'RE FROM THE GOVERNMENT AND WE'RE HERE TO HELP YOU"

At the end of the last chapter, we noted that there are those who call for the government to do something about the "water crisis." What do they want the government to do? And, more important, what has been our experience in the past when government has heeded this call?

Given our experience with price controls on petroleum in the 1970s, we find it hard to believe there are those who today call for price controls. But, there are. As a case in point, look at natural gas. A headline in the *Wall Street Journal* of January 21, 1983, announced that "State Regulators Take Up Battle Against Rising Natural-Gas Prices." Contrary to the mood favoring decontrol that exists within the Reagan administration, some state regulators have begun to fight to block or delay price increases in natural gas. The chairman of Pennsylvania's Public Utility Commission has the opinion that "we're the first line of defense for gas users." It sounds great. And, on political grounds, it might make sense. But from the point of view of avoiding shortages in natural gas, such a policy will be disastrous. Think back to our description of the oil crisis of the 1970s. What happened to us, the consumers, when the federal government "defended" us from high prices that time? The price controls on petroleum led to the shortages we experienced. Will it be any different for natural gas? We think not. A consumer law specialist in the Michigan attorney general's office suggested that in order to hold down the price of natural gas, "states are exploring all the nooks and crannies of the law." We suggest that if this attempt to "protect the consumers" by holding down natural gas prices is successful, the result will be a shortage—a crisis—in natural gas. And the same would be true for any other resource.

As an alternative to price controls, government agencies have in the past tried to eliminate shortages by legislating conservation or directly increasing production. Remember what the U.S. government did with respect to rubber at the beginning of World War II? The Rubber Reserve Company—a government agency—spent $5 million trying unsuccessfully to develop a new source of natural rubber in Brazil. Instead, it was private enterprise that was able to respond to the cut-off of shipments of natural rubber. How about the actions of the U.S. Forest Service during the timber crisis of the early 1900s? Even after the crisis was over, the Forest Service was trying to institute policies that would lead to more planting and growing of trees. As we noted earlier, the Forest Service was tied to a policy of filling the gap without any regard to the impact higher prices would have on the consumption of timber. The net result was that long after the crisis was ended, public expenditures—tax dollars—were being used to finance reforestation that was no longer necessary.

Unfortunately, nothing much has changed since then. During the energy crisis of the 1970s, the U.S. Synthetic Fuels Corporation (SFC) was founded by Congress and was required by law to see that some synthetic fuels were actually produced and marketed. (Note the similarity between this and the filling the gap objective of the Forest Service 70 years earlier.) Once decontrol was accomplished, these synfuels were no longer required. But the law is the law. On December 22, 1982, *The Washington Post* reported that the U.S. Synthetic Fuels Corporation had endorsed backing a plant to produce methanol with loan guarantees of $341 million. Think about that for a moment. After the crisis was long since past and in a period when petroleum prices were falling, the government intended to spend $341 million on a project that its own staff admitted is "economically unpromising." And, unfortunately, that's not all. The SFC would also guarantee a minimum price of $1.05 a gallon for the methanol produced. At the time, methanol was widely available on the Gulf Coast for 50 cents per gallon. The upshot is that the government agency will not only guarantee the loans for an "economically unpromising" project but will also subsidize the output of this project in amounts of 55 cents or more per gallon. According to the newspaper article, total government expenditures could amount to as much as $465 million. Like the Forest Service's plan to reforest, the legal requirement to produce synfuels ignored the marketplace. With this methanol project, we are trying to fill the "gap" that the market eliminated some two years previously.

From the preceding discussion, you can see how we respond to those who argue that the government should do something about resource shortages. The lessons we see in history suggest to us that government programs have been at best wasteful and ineffective and at worst have transformed a shortage into a crisis. To drive the latter point home, permit us to tell you one more story.

A FINAL WARNING

Throughout this book, we have been continually optimistic. We have asserted and our historical examples have demonstrated that if the marketplace is permitted to function freely, shortages will always be eliminated; so economic crises need not lead to doomsday. However, we would be remiss if we left you thinking that there is absolutely nothing to worry about. Economic collapse is indeed possible—an economic doomsday could be in our future. But, and this is the crucial point, our survey of man's history indicates to us that it is only when the marketplace is restrained from operating that shortages can lead to collapse. Put another way, doomsday could arrive; but it would only occur if we invite our own destruction by restricting the ability of the marketplace to function.

As a case in point, let's consider ancient Rome, a civilization we have not yet discussed. When most of us think of Rome, we think of "the glory that was Rome" under Augustus and in the first century A.D. What was responsible for this glory—or, more specifically, the robust economy during the height of Roman civilization? The answer is very simple. A freely functioning market was in place and was working. The emperor Augustus had no special economic policies.

Indeed, many historians point to Rome at this time as an example of laissez-faire policies. If a good became relatively scarce, its price rose; so consumers demanded less, while producers brought more to the market or provided a substitute commodity.

What then led to the collapse of such a strong and vital economy? As Shepard Clough and Richard Rapp have noted, attempts to explain the decline and fall of Rome have been a preoccupation of historians for centuries. In what follows, we do not purport to provide the sole reason for the collapse of Roman civilization. So many conditions contributed that it would be impossible to isolate a single cause of the fall. However, we hope to be able to convince you that the economic policies instituted during the latter period of the empire were definitely a major contributing factor to the collapse—doomsday did come to pass for Rome.

In contrast to the first century, Rome in the third century was a nation faced with numerous problems and shortages. In order to defend the far-flung boundaries of the empire, the state had increased military service requirements and resorted to confiscation of goods. Archaeological evidence indicates that the output of the empire had declined. The roads—the very lifelines of the empire—were deteriorating. (You might find it interesting that the road system built by the ancient Romans totaled 50,000 miles—10,000 miles longer than our own interstate highway system.) The attitude of the people changed from the optimism that had persisted for the past 200 years to sullenness. (Doesn't this all sound very familiar?) Immigration into the empire swelled its population. At the same time, agriculture—the basis of the economy—declined. Land had become more concentrated in great estates. Soil productivity declined. Farmlands in North Africa and elsewhere in the empire deteriorated and were abandoned, due in large part to excessive taxation. Parts of the empire, like North Africa, were so impaired that they were unable to make deliveries of agricultural products. Significantly, some writers have compared Rome's lifeline for grain from Northern Africa to the United States's pipeline for oil from the Middle East.

Faced with these shortages—economic crises—what should the administrators of Rome have done? Our answer would be to let the marketplace work: if there is a shortage of chariots, let the price of chariots rise. With price increases, some consumers would find other means of transportation (perhaps chariot-pooling) and would tend to defer the purchase of a new chariot. At the same time, chariot makers would produce and sell more chariots. Moreover, persons producing other goods would be induced by the higher price to switch to making chariots. (While the example may be stretched, the principle is the same for any commodity.)

Instead, the administrators of Rome did exactly the opposite! Rather than making it easier for the market to function, they virtually eliminated the marketplace. The policies of noninterference by government in the economic life of the empire that had proved so successful under Augustus were abandoned in favor of rigid governmental control. Economic mobility was outlawed. Professions were made hereditary. Likewise, it became illegal to transfer capital from the production of one good to another. Returning to our hypothetical example, how did these restrictions affect the production of chariots? If there was a shortage of chariots, no new producers could enter the market because such entry was prohibited. Hence, the production of chariots would fall and the shortage would be worse.

While the mobility restrictions were bad enough, it was Diocletian, the last of the strong emperors, who finally destroyed the marketplace in Rome. In 301 A.D., he issued an edict for universal wage and price controls. A maximum price was set for every good and service. Maximums were also given for wages, fees, and stipends. The market was eliminated. In our first chapter, we described America's recent experience with price controls on petroleum. Given those experiences, can you imagine the effects of price controls on everything? With price controls, the shortage of chariots we have used as an example would only get worse and worse. Without the price increase, there are no incentives for consumers to conserve or for producers to bring more to the market.

What then were the effects of the mobility restrictions and the wage and price controls on Rome? Productivity, and consequently the standard of living, declined. As J. Donald Hughes of the University of Denver has noted: "One of Rome's lasting virtues [had been] her ability to fill the ranks of an enfeebled and shrinking ruling class with vigorous, intelligent people from the lower classes and from other nationalities within the Roman sphere." Mobility restrictions ended that. Where was the incentive to work harder or to innovate? Some free men even elected to become slaves, reasoning that it was better to be a slave (with someone else responsible for room and board) than to try to make a living in such a controlled state. Customers became fewer. Many large industrial concerns disappeared, while others were transferred to state ownership. The economy was dying.

Although historians date the end of Rome with the retirement of the last emperor in 476 A.D., Rome as a major civilization had died much earlier. Given the economic conditions we have described, do you feel it is necessary to point to the "barbarians from the north" in order to explain the fall of Rome? We do not. To us, it is apparent that Rome invited the collapse by suspending the marketplace.

Therein lies our warning. We have shown you several examples of how economic crises have been eliminated by letting the market work. Now we have shown how an economic crisis contributed to the collapse of a civilization because the market was not permitted to function. Today and in the future we will again face that choice.

SOURCES

CHAPTER 1

American Petroleum Institute. *Basic Petroleum Data Book*. January 1983.

Chapman, Stephen. "The Gas Lines of '79." *Public Interest*, Summer 1980.

Griffin, James M., and Steele, Henry B. *Energy Economics and Policy*. New York: Academic Press, 1980.

Howard, Frank A. *Buna Rubber: The Birth of an Industry*. New York: D. Van Nostrand Co., 1947.

Meadows, Donella H.; Meadows, Dennis L.; Randers, Jørgen; and Behrens, William W., III. *The Limits to Growth*. New York: Universe Books, 1972.

Tucker, William. "The Energy Crisis Is Over!" *Harper's*, November 1981.

U.S. Department of Energy. *Monthly Energy Review*, January 1983.

CHAPTER 2

Ekelund, Robert B., and Herbert, Robert F. *A History of Economic Theory and Method*. New York: McGraw-Hill, 1975.

KUED, Salt Lake City. "The Doomsayers," produced for the Public Broadcasting System, 1981.

Peccei, Aurelio. *One Hundred Pages for the Future*. New York: New American Library, 1982.

Roll, Eric. *A History of Economic Thought.* Englewood Cliffs, N.J.: Prentice-Hall, 1953.

Simon, Julian. "Should We Heed the Prophets of Doom?" *Science Digest,* October 1983.

Smith, Adam. *An Inquiry into the Nature and Causes of the Wealth of Nations.* Edited by C. J. Bullock. The Harvard Classics, Vol. 10. New York: Collier, 1937, 1961.

CHAPTER 3

Haynes, William, and Hauser, Ernest A. *Rationed Rubber.* New York: Alfred A. Knopf, 1942.

Howard, Frank A. *Buna Rubber: The Birth of an Industry.* New York: D. Van Nostrand Co., 1947.

Knorr, K. E. *World Rubber and Its Regulation.* Stanford, Calif.: Stanford University Press, 1945.

Phillips, Charles F., Jr. *Competition in the Synthetic Rubber Industry.* Chapel Hill: University of North Carolina Press, 1961.

CHAPTER 4

Olson, Sherry H. *The Depletion Myth.* Cambridge, Mass.: Harvard University Press, 1971.

Rosenberg, Nathan. "Innovative Responses to Materials Shortages." *American Economic Review* 62 (1972): 111–18.

CHAPTER 5

Burton, Robert. *The Life and Death of Whales.* 2nd ed. New York: Universe Books, 1980.

"The Emergence of Order out of Chaos." *World Oil* (centennial issue), January 1959.

Forbes, R. J. *Studies in Early Petroleum History.* Leiden, Netherlands: E. J. Brill, 1958.

Giddens, Paul H. *The Birth of the Oil Industry.* New York: Macmillan, 1938.

———. *Pennsylvania Petroleum, 1750–1872.* Titusville: Pennsylvania Historical and Museum Commission, 1947.

Hohman, E. P. *The American Whalesman*. New York: Longmans, Green, and Co., 1928.

Ommanney, F. D. *Lost Leviathan*. New York: Dodd, Mead, and Co., 1971.

Shuman, Roland B. *The Petroleum Industry*. Norman: University of Oklahoma Press, 1940.

Starbuck, Alexander. *History of the American Whale Fishery*. New York: Argosy-Antiquarian, 1964.

Tower, Walter A. *A History of the American Whale Fishery*. Philadelphia: John C. Winston Co., 1907.

Verrill, A. H. *The Real Story of the Whaler*. New York: D. Appleton and Co., 1916.

Whipple, A. B. C. *The Whalers*. Alexandria, Va.: Time-Life Books, 1979.

Williamson, Harold F., and Daum, Arnold R. *The American Petroleum Industry: The Age of Illumination, 1859–1899*. Evanston, Ill.: Northwestern University Press, 1959.

CHAPTER 6

Boserup, Ester. *Population and Technological Change*. Chicago: University of Chicago Press, 1981.

Clough, Shepard B., and Rapp, Richard T. *European Economic History*. 3rd ed. New York: McGraw-Hill, 1975.

Clow, Archibald, and Clow, Nan L. *The Chemical Revolution*. London: Batchworth Press, 1952.

Nef, John U. "An Early Energy Crisis and Its Consequences." *Scientific American*, November 1977.

———. *The Rise of the British Coal Industry*. London: George Routledge & Sons, 1932.

CHAPTER 7

Anderson, J. E., trans. *Land and Work in Medieval Europe: Selected Papers of Marc Bloch*. Berkeley and Los Angeles: University of California Press, 1967.

Boserup, Ester. *Population and Technological Change*. Chicago: University of Chicago Press, 1981.

Clough, Shepard B., and Rapp, Richard T. *European Economic History*. 3rd ed. New York: McGraw-Hill, 1975.

Finn, Rex Weldon. *Domesday Book: A Guide.* London: Phillmore, 1973.

Gelman, Judith R. "The English Economy Following the Black Death." Federal Trade Commission, Bureau of Economics Working Paper no. 80. Washington, D.C., November 1982.

Langer, William L. "The Black Death. " *Scientific American,* February 1964.

Leonardo da Vinci. *Notebooks.* Trans., arranged, and introduced by Edward MacCurdy. New York: G. Braziller, 1955.

Lipson, Ephraim. *The Economic History of England: The Middle Ages.* Vol. 1. London: Adam and Charles Black, 1947.

McGary, Daniel. *Medieval History and Civilization.* New York: Macmillan, 1976.

Miskimin, Harry. *The Economy of Early Renaissance Europe, 1300–1460.* Cambridge, Eng.: Cambridge University Press, 1975.

North, Douglass C., and Thomas, Robert Paul. *The Rise of the Western World.* Cambridge, Eng.: Cambridge University Press, 1973.

Postan, M. M., and Rich, E. E., eds. *The Cambridge Economic History of Europe.* Cambridge, Eng.: Cambridge University Press, 1952.

White, Lynn, Jr. *Medieval Technology and Social Change.* London: Oxford University Press, 1962.

Ziegler, Philip. *The Black Death.* New York: Harper and Row, 1969.

CHAPTER 8

Bass, George F. "Tales from an Ancient Ship," in *Odyssey,* a program guide for the "Odyssey" television series. Boston: Public Broadcasting Associates.

Bass, George F., ed. *A History of Seafaring Based on Underwater Archaeology.* New York: Walker and Co., 1972.

Casson, Lionel. *Ships and Seamanship in the Ancient World.* Princeton, N.J.: Princeton University Press, 1971.

Homer, *The Odyssey.* Trans. by Ennis Rees. Indianapolis, Ind.: Bobbs-Merrill Educational Publishing, 1977.

Snodgrass, Anthony M. *The Dark Age of Greece.* Edinburgh: Edinburgh University Press, 1971.

Waldbaum, Jane C. *From Bronze to Iron: Studies in Mediterranean Archaeology.* Vol. 54. Goteborg, Sweden: P. Astrom, 1978.

Wertime, Theodore A., and Muhly, James D., eds. *The Coming of the Age of Iron*. New Haven, Conn.: Yale University Press, 1980.

CHAPTER 9

Bender, Barbara. *Farming in Prehistory: From Hunter-Gatherer to Food-Producer*. New York: St. Martin's Press, 1975.

Binford, Lewis R. "Post-Pleistocene Adaptations." In Sally R. Binford and Lewis R. Binford, eds., *New Perspectives in Archaeology*. Chicago, Ill: Aldine Publishing Co., 1968.

Flannery, Kent V. "Origins and Ecological Effects of Early Domestication in Iran and the Near East." In Peter J. Ucko and G. W. Dimbleby, eds., *The Domestication and Exploitation of Plants and Animals*. London: Gerald Duckworth and Co., 1969.

Hester, Thomas R., ed. "The Colha Project, 1979: A Collection of Interim Papers." San Antonio: University of Texas, Center for Archaeological Research, July 1979.

Shafer, Harry J. "The Lithic Artifacts of the Pulltrouser Area: Settlements and Fields." In B. L. Turner, II and Peter D. Harrison, eds., *Pulltrouser Swamp: Ancient Maya Habitat, Culture, and Settlement in Northern Belize*. Pan American Series. Austin: University of Texas Press, 1983.

Shafer, Harry J., and Hester, Thomas R. "Ancient Maya Chert Workshops in Northern Belize, Central America." *American Antiquity* 48 (1983).

Turner, B. L., II; Harrison, Peter D.; Fry, Robert E.; Ettlinger, Nancy; Darch, Janice P.; Johnson, William C.; Shafer, Harry J.; Covich, Alan; Wiseman, Frederick M.; and Miksicek, Charles. "Maya Raised–Field Agriculture and Settlement at Pulltrouser Swamp, Northern Belize." Report of the 1979–80 University of Oklahoma–National Science Foundation Pulltrouser Swamp Project.

CHAPTER 10

Heimes, F. J., and Luckey, R. R. "Method for Estimating Historical Requirements for Ground Water in the High Plains in Parts of Colo, Kansas, Nebraska, New Mexico, Oklahoma, South Dakota, Texas, and Wyoming." Water Resources Investigations Report 82–40. Denver, Colo.: U.S. Geological Survey, 1982.

Nieswisdomy, Michael L. "Adjusting to Diminishing Water Supplies in Irrigated Agriculture." Ph.D. dissertation, Texas A&M University, 1983.

CHAPTER 11

Clough, Shepard B., and Rapp, Richard T. *European Economic History*, 3rd ed. New York: McGraw-Hill, 1975.

Hughes, J. Donald. *Ecology in Ancient Civilizations*. Albuquerque: University of New Mexico Press, 1975.

Rostovtsev, M. *Social and Economic History of the Roman Empire*. Vol. 1. Oxford: Clarendon Press, 1957.

Starr, Chester G. *A History of the Ancient World*. New York: Oxford University Press, 1974.